The Acheulian Site of Gesher Benot Ya'aqov, Israel
The Wood Assemblage

Aerial view of the Gesher Benot Ya'aqov site.

The Acheulian Site of Gesher Benot Ya'aqov, Israel The Wood Assemblage

Naama Goren-Inbar

Institute of Archaeology
The Hebrew University of Jerusalem
Jerusalem, Israel

Ella Werker

Department of Botany
The Hebrew Uinversity of Jerusalem
Jerusalem, Israel

Craig S. Feibel

Departments of Anthropology and Geological Sciences
Rutgers University
New Brunswick, New Jersey, USA

Oxbow Books

The Acheulian Site of Gesher Benot Ya'aqov, Israel
Series Editor: Naama Goren-Inbar

Published by
Oxbow Books, Park End Place, Oxford OX1 1HN

© Oxbow Books and the individual authors, 2002

ISBN 1 84217 072 4

A CIP record for this book is available from The British Library

This book is available direct from
Oxbow Books, Park End Place, Oxford OX1 1HN
(Phone: 01865-241249; Fax: 01865-794449)

and
The David Brown Book Company
PO Box 511, Oakville, CT 06779, USA
(Phone: 860-945-9329; Fax: 860-945-9468)

and from our website:
www.oxbowbooks.com

Cover design and layout: Noah Lichtinger

Printed in Great Britain at
The Short Run Press, Exeter

Table of Contents

Foreword

The Acheulian (or 'handaxe') cultural tradition began in Africa about 1.6 million years ago, and for the next million years or so, it was apparently confined to Africa and south-western Asia. About 600,000 years ago, handaxe makers of African descent reached Europe, where they became the first colonists to hang on through thick and thin, or more precisely, through warm and cold. The Acheulian tradition persisted in Africa, western Asia, and Europe until 250–200,000 years ago, the exact time perhaps depending on the place.

Our understanding of human behaviour during the long Acheulian time span remains dim. More than 150 years after scholars first recognized handaxes as ancient artefacts, we still know little about how handaxes were used. The best guess is that they were multipurpose tools or Palaeolithic Swiss Army knives that could be turned to hunting, butchering, plant collection, wood-working, or many other essential tasks. It is often said that the handaxes and accompanying stone artefacts changed little during the long Acheulian interval, yet Later Acheulian people frequently produced more thoroughly flaked, thinner, and symmetrical handaxes, and they also made sophisticated flake tools like those of their Middle Stone Age successors in sub-Saharan Africa or their Middle Palaeolithic successors in northern Africa, western Asia, and Europe. In addition, to manufacture flake tools, Later Acheulian people honed the Levallois technique for predetermining the size and shape of a flake before it was removed from the core. Future research may show that there was a relatively abrupt shift from the earlier to the later Acheulian around 600,000 years ago, coinciding with a relatively abrupt increase in brain size to about 90% of the modern average. Such a linked change in technology and intellectual capacity could account for the first permanent colonization of Europe.

Like all humans until roughly 11,000 years ago, Acheulian people were hunter-gatherers, but little is known about their hunting-and-gathering capacity. Observations at some African and European sites suggest that they acquired large animals infrequently, and it seems likely that their populations were small. In their ability to extract energy from nature, they may have been advanced over yet earlier (Oldowan) people, but it seems likely that they were less capable than their successors, particularly than those who lived after 50,000 years ago. These latter people, whom archaeologists refer to the Later Stone Age in sub-Saharan Africa and to the Upper Palaeolithic in northern Africa, western Asia, and Europe were the first to match historic hunter-gatherers in every detectable aspect of material culture.

One reason why the Acheulian Tradition is so poorly understood is that despite its long time span and enormous geographic range, it is known from fewer than twenty-five excavated localities where handaxes and other artefacts are sealed in ancient deposits with animal or plant fossils that can illuminate ancient behaviour and ecology. Among the known occurrences, none is more informative than Gesher Benot Ya'aqov in the Dead Sea Rift of Israel, where Naama Goren-Inbar supervised systematic excavations between 1989 and 1997. Goren-Inbar's team recovered thousands of Acheulian artefacts and animal bones that accumulated in and around an ancient lake about 780,000 years ago. The deposits have remained waterlogged virtually ever since, and this unusual circumstance resulted in the preservation of plant macrofossils, including pieces of wood and bark that can be identified to species. Most of the pieces probably accumulated naturally around the lake, but the excavators recovered one willow fragment that Acheulian people had transformed into a flat, plank-like object. It is probably the oldest wooden artefact yet discovered. They also found an oak log from which ancient people had apparently stripped the side branches, perhaps to produce a lever with which they could overturn the skull of a dead elephant nearby.

In contrast to pollen, which is far more durable and thus commonly occurs in ancient sites (including Gesher Benot Ya'aqov), wood and bark fragments are more likely to have originated nearby, and they thus reveal the local (versus the regional) vegetation. In this monograph, Goren-Inbar and her colleagues describe the geological and archaeological context of the ancient wood, the criteria for its identification, and its implications for the surroundings of Gesher Benot Ya'aqov in Acheulian times. They also provide a welcome survey of the wood fragments that have occasionally been found at other ancient Palaeolithic sites. In future volumes, Goren-Inbar's team will describe the abundant artefacts, bones, and other plant fossils from Gesher Benot Ya'aqov, and the result, following on this thorough account and analysis of the wood, will be a rich data trove that archaeologists can mine as they seek to reduce the mysteries that have long shrouded the Acheulian.

Richard G. Klein
Program in Human Biology
Stanford University

Preface

The discovery of ancient wood fragments during the first field season at the Acheulian site of Gesher Benot Ya'aqov came as a shock. They were large (it later turned out that these were the largest pieces excavated at the site) and looked like pieces of darkish modern wood, soft and waterlogged. While previous archaeological experience was instrumental in dealing with problems of tilted strata, exposure of large fossil bone specimens and handling complex stratigraphic problems, it was inadequate for the recovery of waterlogged wood segments from the Acheulian occupations of the Benot Ya'akov Formation. The high temperatures, strong sunlight, evaporation and other climatic factors had to be dealt with immediately, along with photographing, cataloguing, storage and transportation. A search for expert assistance was immediately carried out and resulted in the involvement of Ms. Orna Cohen, archaeologist and conservationist. Her vast knowledge and good will were of tremendous help both on the site and later on during years of continued conservation treatment. A slow learning process began then in the field, accompanied by the accumulation of experience during later field seasons and by constant improvisation. The result was a wood assemblage unique in the Levant for its antiquity and completeness.

All the above was carried out with the feeling that the team was enormously fortunate to be excavating wood assemblages from Lower/Middle Pleistocene deposits. The scarcity of material of this kind assigned to such an early date in the Levant and the opportunity to participate in this process turned the excavation into an educational experience accompanied by a sense of immense responsibility. When archaeology explores the unknown and encounters the unpredictable, the difficult and strenuous work becomes a pleasure.

The present Gesher Benot Ya'aqov volume is dedicated to the wood assemblage from the site and will be followed by a series of studies each focusing on a different aspect of the multidisciplinary investigations. In this work, the Introduction reviews the geographical, climatological and geological background of the Hula Valley and of the archaeological site. The history of research at the site is described, as are the objectives of the present study. Methodology is concerned with the excavation techniques in general and with the complete treatment of the wood fragments (excavation, transportation and conservation) in particular. The tectonically deformed strata of the Benot Ya'akov Formation necessitate a unique approach and excavation techniques to handle the recovery of artefacts and contextual data. The presence of the waterlogged wood segments required entirely different excavation and storage processes. A similar strategy was also applied to the large quantity of disintegrating basalt artefacts. The Geology chapter offers a background for understanding the wood's environment of deposition as well as some data on the chronological assignment of the formation and the wood assemblage embedded in it. The Wood Anatomy section is the backbone of this volume. It offers, for the first time, an insight into the anatomical characteristics of a Levantine wood assemblage of Lower/ Middle Pleistocene age. It includes detailed anatomical descriptions of the characteristics of the identified taxa, the present habitats of the identified plant species, and the inferred habitats of the GBY woods. This chapter is also concerned with the extinct species discovered at GBY and with the limitations of identification by wood anatomy. The Wood Taphonomy chapter attempts to explain the mechanisms which resulted in the deposition of the wood segments in the Benot Ya'akov Formation deposits. It offers several hypotheses and examines them in the light of the archaeological, geological and climatological evidence. The chapter integrates subjects such as the size and spatial organization of the wood. It discusses the hypothesis that the wood was driftwood and postulates a particular drainage model as an explanation of the entire wood assemblage at the site. The chapter on Wooden Artefacts is descriptive and concerns the small number of artefacts recognized from the site. The Burned Wood chapter examines the specimens of burnt wood recovered in the excavations and their implications. The Discussion attempts an integrative approach to all of the previous data. It also includes a short discussion of the minimal presence of wooden tools/artefacts from various cultural entities assigned to the Lower Palaeolithic. Finally, the discussion reviews the contribution of the wood assemblage to the palaeoecology of the ancient Hula Valley and its implications for the hominins that occupied this region in antiquity.

And finally, a very personal word: directing a large-scale multidisciplinary project has many advantages and disadvantages. It was a stroke of good fortune that I learned of the high academic qualifications of Dr. Ella Werker, and she willingly integrated her vast knowledge of wood anatomy into the project of Gesher Benot Ya'aqov. Working together on this task for many years has been a great pleasure, both academically and personally. It was her outstanding scholarly qualifications and good nature that enabled the publication of this monograph. I owe her many thanks.

N. G.-I.
Jerusalem, February 2002

Acknowledgements

The field and laboratory work reported here was carried out with grants from the L.S.B. Leakey Foundation, the National Geographic Society (USA) and the Irene Levi–Sala Care Archeological Foundation. The Israel Science Foundation and the Hebrew University of Jerusalem also supported the laboratory work. All the wood conservation and restoration was continuously supported by special grants of the Irene Levi–Sala Care Archeological Foundation. This (always tight) budget permitted us to carry out the excavations, but the assistance, guidance, enthusiasm and growing expertise of the team actually enabled the progress of this aspect of the excavation.

It was the students, colleagues and participants who made the current study possible. Special thanks are due to the following individuals who assisted in different ways in the process of cleaning, cataloguing and conserving the wood segments. This help took place in the field and in the laboratory, in the evenings, after many long and strenuous working hours. The following individuals were directly involved with the wood fragments: O. Cohen, I. Saragusti, H. Taub, M. Wiseman, O. Marder, T. Vitelzon and P. Enamorado-Rivero. J. Berg helped to establish the site grid. Special thanks are due to Y. Arbel and H. Milrad, members of Kibbutz Gadot, for their continuous help through the years. Members of this kibbutz, which lodged the expedition, provided outstanding hospitality and shared our enthusiasm. Others, whose names are too numerous to be mentioned here, contributed to the present volume.

The complex process of wood conservation was undertaken by O. Cohen. We thank her for her efforts and for the summary of conservation methods that appears in Chapter 2.

The rarity of wood finds of such antiquity brought up the issue of museology, leading to an investment of time, expertise and funds that culminated in the production of a series of casts of a small selection of wood segments. O. Cohen and M. Chech (CNRS, France) handled this complex procedure very successfully. They worked zealously and produced excellent casts (exhibited in Israel and abroad) of great precision and authenticity which can be the subject of detailed studies in the future.

The Israel Plant Information Centre, Centre for Documentation, Research and Education of the Flowers of Israel (ROTEM: a joint project of the Hebrew University of Jerusalem and the Society for the Protection of Nature) allowed us to use some of their data that relate to the present study. These data were handled by T. Shamir and B. Levinson and processed with the help of the Hebrew University GIS unit, with the outstanding and constant help of A. Ben-Nun. These data were further improved graphically by T. Sopher. Technical, storage and administrative help were provided by the Director of the Institute of Archaeology, B. Sekay. Data on the climate of the Hula Valley were kindly supplied by the Israel Meteorological Service.

S. Lev-Yadun generously refereed an early version of the present study; his help is much appreciated. S. Gorodetsky edited the manuscript and helped immensely in making it clear and coherent, for which we are most grateful.

S. Halbreich drew Figures 25, 26 and C. Douzil Figure 6. T. Vitelzon drew Figure 18 (field sketch) and R. Burns Figure 20 (field sketch). Computerized graphics were prepared by G. Hivroni (Figures 2– 5), E. Amsalem and T. Sopher (Figures 10–16, 22 and 27) and V. Shatil (Figures 23, 24). P. Grosman produced Figures 7–9 and R. Bonfil Figure 17. N. Lichtinger produced many and made a great contribution to all of the computerized graphics.

Photographs 1-14, 29–32 were taken by S. Lev-Yadun, who also contributed to the microscope photography, as did E. Werker. G. Laron, the director of the laboratory of photography at the Institute of Archaeology, invested many working days in achieving good results from extremely difficult hand-sectioned slides. Photographs 15–18, 22 and 31 are his, as well as the development of his photographs and those taken by E. Werker and S. Lev-Yadun. A. Baltinester took the photograph on the frontispiece.

M. Jaggo kindly illustrated his views (below) on the edible component of the plant material…

N. Lichtinger designed and produced the book creatively.

The authors thank David Brown of Oxbow Books for providing the opportunity to publish the Gesher Benot Ya'aqov series of which the present monograph is the first volume.

List of Tables

List of Figures

List of Photographs

List of Plates

Chapter 1 – Introduction

'North of the lake is an extensive marsh, covered with canes and flags, into which nothing can penetrate. This marsh extends westward, and north-westward in some places, along the streams which enter it from that quarter…'

(Robinson, 1865: 68-69)

'On the south the basin of the Hûleh is closed by a broad tract of uneven and mostly uncultivated higher ground which shelves down from the base of the loftier hills around Safed, and shuts up the whole valley; leaving only a depression south of the lake, along which the Jordan rushes, in its deep and rocky chasm, to the lake of Tiberias…'.

(Robinson, 1865: 69)

Between 1989 and 1997 an intensive research effort was undertaken at the site of Gesher Benot Ya'aqov in Israel. The wide scope of this research makes a great contribution to the study of palaeoenvironments and hominin behaviour in an Acheulian site located within the Dead Sea Rift System, in the sector termed the 'Levantine Corridor' (Tchernov, 1988; 1992; Thomas, 1985). This corridor is considered to be one of several possible routes through which biotic exchange took place between Africa and Eurasia. The 'Out of Africa' model, which views the spread of *Homo erectus* from the African continent into other parts of the Old World as a dispersal from one palaeogeographical domain to another, views this corridor as one of the most likely routes employed.

It is in the Levantine sector of the Dead Sea Rift that the most ancient non-African archaeological evidence exists, deriving mainly from two Palaeolithic sites: the older is that of 'Ubeidiya and the younger, that of Gesher Benot Ya'aqov. Both sites are bedded in Pleistocene formations and they are both assigned to the Acheulian Industrial Complex. Each comprises a substantial sequence of archaeological occurrences located on palaeo-lake shores and their vicinity. The site of 'Ubeidiya is dated to 1.4 Ma (Bar-Yosef and Goren-Inbar, 1993; Tchernov, 1987) and that of Gesher Benot Ya'aqov to 0.78 Ma (Goren-Inbar et al., 2000; Verosub et al., 1998). At 'Ubeidiya more than 70 archaeological occurrences are known, all bedded in a 179 m thick sedimentary sequence (Bar-Yosef and Goren-Inbar, 1993). The site of Gesher Benot Ya'aqov is known from a 34 m thick sequence (Feibel et al., 1998) in which at least

seven archaeological horizons are present (Goren-Inbar, 1998). Each of these sites yielded thousands of *in situ* stone artefacts within a thoroughly investigated stratigraphic sequence. Indeed, our understanding of ancient hominins and their activities in these Levantine sites is based primarily on the archaeological record and the contexts of the sites, since the hominin fossils from these sites provide minimal information. The meagre osteological evidence of hominins from 'Ubeidiya is inadequate for definite species identification (Tobias, 1966). At Gesher Benot Ya'aqov too the only extant hominin remains were found out of context and the osteological elements (two femurs) do not permit a definite conclusion regarding the bones' antiquity (Geraads and Tchernov, 1983) or assignment to an archaic hominin species.

Excavations at the site of 'Ubeidiya have contributed an extraordinary wealth of data on Lower Pleistocene fauna, comprising an extremely diversified and abundant palaeontological assemblage that includes hundreds of species originating in different palaeogeographical regions, as well as many endemic ones (Tchernov, 1986). Excavations at Gesher Benot Ya'aqov also yielded a rich palaeontological data set, most of which is still under investigation (but see Goren-Inbar et al., 1994; Goren-Inbar et al., 2000). Though the large mammal assemblages differ between the two sites and they are assigned to different biostratigraphic time units, the existence of such diverse mammalian communities in the Dead Sea Rift, together with their association with early hominins, generates a wide range of questions regarding the ancient environments and habitats of the region.

The vegetation of the region during Lower and Middle Pleistocene times must have been rich enough to sustain large herbivorous animals such as elephants, rhinos, aurochs, hippos and others (Goren-Inbar et al., 1992b; Goren-Inbar et al., 1994). The present ecological conditions could not provide the quantities of food needed by these ancient animals. The change is due in great part to the intervention of modern man. However, changes in climate and ecological conditions may also have been responsible for a change in vegetation, both qualitative and quantitative. Plant species that are currently extinct may have grown in the region at that time and new wild species may have been introduced since then. Examination of plant remains may, at least partly, provide answers to these questions.

Reconstructions of the behaviour of Acheulian hominins are largely based on present-day African environments and to a much lesser extent on fossil data retrieved in excavations. These models are relevant to the African continent, but 'Out of Africa' models that are concerned with the dispersal of hominin groups require data from outside that continent. The Gesher Benot Ya'aqov plant data that are discussed in this study contribute much to attempts to reconstruct the particular palaeoenvironmental conditions within the Dead Sea Rift ecological zone.

A major difference between most studies of previously excavated sites and the present study is in the age and character of the wood assemblages. Most of the archaeological assemblages that have yielded palaeobotanical remains (e.g. Albert et al., 1999; 2000; Schiegl et al., 1994) are associated with intensive food gathering, storage, hearths, building materials and the production of special items (ornaments, utensils, etc.). The unique contribution of the Gesher Benot Ya'aqov palaeobotanical assemblage lies in its great antiquity of some 780,000 years (Goren-Inbar et al., 2000; Verosub et al., 1998) and its potential value for palaeoenvironmental reconstruction of a pre-agricultural age that predates changes induced by intensive human activities. It relates to hominin groups of hunter-gatherers living in a rich ecological niche, exploiting but not destroying its potential (Goren-Inbar et al., 2002).

The goals of this volume are to report on the detailed morphological, taxonomic and ecological analyses of the Gesher Benot Ya'aqov wood assemblage, to place the wood assemblage in its stratigraphic, depositional and taphonomic context and to use the wood data as a basis for reconstructing aspects of ancient environments in and around the ancient Hula Basin. The results of this study are of significance for study of the rich archaeological assemblages of Gesher Benot Ya'aqov, the palaeoecology of the hominins who were active at the site, the community ecology of the Pleistocene Jordan Rift, and regional analyses of environmental character and change in the Levant.

The Hula Valley Today

The site of Gesher Benot Ya'aqov is located in the northern sector of the Dead Sea Rift (Horowitz, 2001). It lies within the northern part of the Jordan Valley, known as the Hula Valley. This region (Figure 1) is bordered by the rift escarpments in the east (Golan Heights) and west (Naftali Mountains), which rise to 500–1000 m above sea level (asl). Two landform barriers delimit the Hula Valley within the rift: the Iyoun valley and the flanking Hermon range (up to 2800 m asl) in the north, and the elevated basaltic block of Korazim (up to 300 m asl) in the west and south.

The Hula Valley is a long, narrow region (25 km long and 6–8 km wide) which is flat and has an average elevation of 90 m asl. The southern sector was occupied by the shallow Lake Hula (1400 hectares) until it was drained in the 1950s (Dimentman et al., 1992; Karmon,

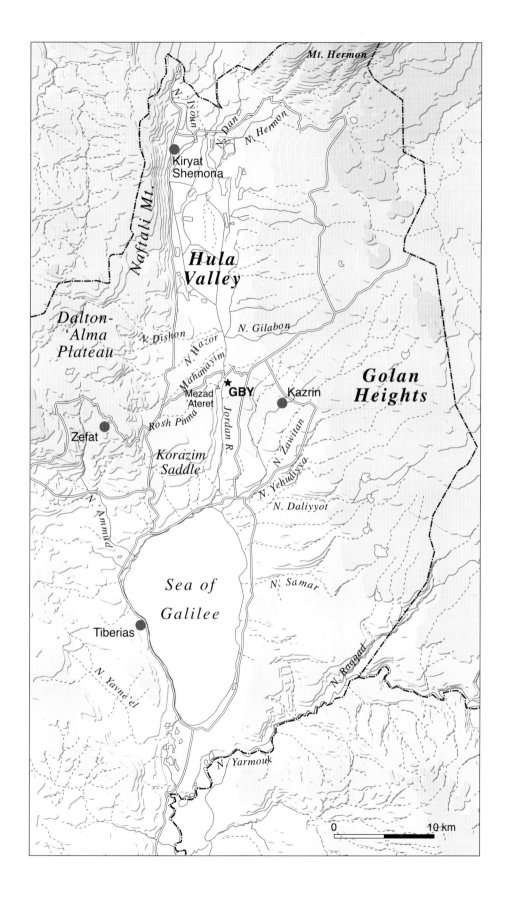

Figure 1: Location map of the upper Jordan Valley (the Hula Valley and vicinity).

1960). The central part of the valley is covered by peat and lignite deposits resulting from rich organic material growing in the swamps (3100 hectares) (Karmon, 1960). The northern part, slightly more elevated, is covered by alluvial soils and crossed by several streams which supply water to the whole of the Jordan Valley (Belitzky, 1987; Horowitz, 1979; Karmon, 1953).

Climate

The climate of the Hula Valley is a warm Mediterranean one due to its geographical setting and relatively low elevation. It is characterized by a hot dry summer and a cool rainy winter. The maximum summer temperature is 40°C, while during winter the temperature may drop below 0°C. The mean annual temperature is 21°C (Gat and Paster, 1974). Tables 1–3 present climatological averages. Yearly precipitation in the valley ranges from 400 to 800 mm (Karmon 1960; Gat and Paster, 1974; 1975). Table 3 illustrates the measured annual precipitation at two geographically close localities in the valley. It is worth noting that despite the short distance between the two localities there is a large difference in the annual

Table 1: Temperature (°C) measured at Kibbutz Kefar Blum in 1977–1979.

Month	I	II	III	IV	V	VI	VII	VIII	IX	X	XI	XII
Average daily maximum	16.4	18.5	21.2	25.1	29.6	32.3	33.3	33.4	32.6	30.0	24.5	18.0
Daily average	11.0	12.4	14.6	17.8	21.3	24.2	25.7	25.8	24.6	21.6	17.2	12.5
Average daily minimum	5.7	6.3	8.1	10.6	13.2	16.1	18.0	18.2	16.7	13.2	9.8	6.9
Average daily range	10.7	12.2	13.1	14.5	16.4	16.2	15.3	15.2	15.9	16.8	14.7	11.1
Average monthly maximum	22.8	24.7	29.4	34.8	38.5	39.4	37.5	37.6	38.4	36.7	30.8	25.5
Absolute maximum	26.5	30.7	35.8	38.5	42.0	42.3	42.1	41.7	41.7	40.6	34.8	29.2
Average monthly minimum	0.3	0.9	1.9	5.1	8.5	12.5	15.0	15.4	12.9	8.8	4.0	1.2
Absolute minimum	-3.8	-3.4	-1.0	1.9	6.3	10.3	13.6	12.5	10.9	5.2	-0.8	-2.6

Table 2: Relative humidity (%) measured at Kibbutz Kefar Blum in 1977–1979.

Month	I	II	III	IV	V	VI	VII	VIII	IX	X	XI	XII
Daily average	70	68	64	59	53	54	59	62	59	58	62	71
Average at												
08:00	83	83	75	65	58	58	63	67	67	68	74	84
14:00	54	48	44	39	33	34	39	40	37	35	40	53
20:00	76	73	70	65	58	57	62	67	67	69	70	77
Average daily maximum	91	91	87	83	77	77	81	86	84	85	87	93
Average daily minimum	50	45	41	36	29	31	38	39	35	32	37	50

Table 3: Average annual precipitation (1961–1990 Sept. to May).
a) Kibbutz Kefar Blum

Month	I	II	III	IV	V	VI	VII	VIII	IX	X	XI	XII	Annual Average
in mm	122	95	74	31	8	0.6	0	0	0	22	64	107	524

b) Yesod Ha'maalah

Month	I	II	III	IV	V	VI	VII	VIII	IX	X	XI	XII	Annual Average
in mm	106	76	59	25	6	0	0	0	1.5	16	54	92	435

precipitation averages, which decline southwards. Additional climatological information on the prevailing wind directions in the Hula Valley will be presented in Chapter 5.

Vegetation

The Hula Valley lies within the Mediterranean phytogeographical zone (Zohary, 1959; 1962). A large part of Lake Hula and the marshes surrounding it was artificially drained in 1951–1959. Today most of the region comprises cultivated and fallow land. The wild vegetation accordingly consists mainly of segetal plants (associated with cultivated sites) and ruderal plants (inhabiting waste places near habitations). Among the segetal vegetation on the alluvial plain are scattered dwarf shrubs of *Prosopis farcta* (screw bean) (Zohary and Orshansky, 1947). Along water margins grow trees of *Salix* (willow) (Photos 1, 2) and scattered trees of *Fraxinus syriaca* (ash) (Photo 3). On dry land there are scattered trees of *Quercus ithaburensis* (Tabor oak) (Photos 4, 5) and *Pistacia atlantica* (Atlantic terebinth) (Photos 6, 7). On the border of the plain, *Ziziphus spina-christi* (jujube) (Photo 8) and *Z. lotus* (lotus thorn) are quite common. The latter two are considered late newcomers that penetrated no earlier than the devastation of the climax flora of the valley. This climax

Photo 2: *Salix*.

Photo 3: *Fraxinus syriaca*.

Photo 1: *Salix*.

Photo 4: *Quercus ithaburensis*.

Photo 5: *Quercus ithaburensis.*

Photo 7: *Pistacia atlantica.*

Photo 9: *Quercus calliprinos.*

Photo 6: *Pistacia atlantica.*

Photo 8: *Ziziphus.*

flora of the border was most likely the *Quercus ithaburensis – Pistacia atlantica* association (Zohary and Orshansky, 1947).

Fraxinus syriaca is concentrated today mainly along the Dan Valley in the north, together with *Salix acmophylla* (common willow). *Quercus ithaburensis* accompanied by *Pistacia atlantica* grow on the slopes of the Golan adjacent to the Hula Valley in the east, in the Dan Valley, and in Upper and Lower Galilee. *Quercus ithaburensis* also grows in stands on the basalt of Korazim in the west and south. *Ulmus canescens* (hairy elm) grows in shady creeks by water in Lower Galilee (Zohary, 1966). An association of *Quercus calliprinos* (Kermes oak) (Photo 9) – *Pistacia palaestina* (Palestine terebinth) is dominant in the mountains of Galilee west of the valley (Zohary, 1960).

The Site

The Acheulian site of Gesher Benot Ya'aqov (henceforth GBY) is located some four kilometres south of the Hula Valley, in the bed and on both banks of the Jordan River (33° 00' 30" N, 35° 37' 30" E). The site is flanked by the Golan Heights to the east, the 'Korazim Saddle' to the west and south, and the Hula Valley to the north (Figure 1). Its elevation is some 70 m asl (Goren-Inbar and Belitzky, 1989). The site is currently known to extend for about 3.5 km along the Jordan River on its north-south axis, but its east-west axis is minimally exposed.

GBY is a wet site. The sedimentary layers, together with the artefacts, fauna and flora included in them, have been waterlogged since their deposition. The palaeo-Lake Hula was one factor contributing to the high water table. More recently, the proximity of the perennial Jordan River, as well as the abundant springs which issue from between basalt flows of the Golan, has kept the site wet. The persistence of saturated conditions at the site has resulted in unusually good preservation conditions for the lithic artefacts and the organic remains reported here. This preservation is a major aspect of GBY's uniqueness.

The site has been archaeologically known from the early 1930s and has been excavated by several expeditions since then. From 1989 excavations were resumed at a locality situated immediately south of the Benot Ya'aqov bridges (Figure 2), a project directed by Naama Goren-Inbar on behalf of the Institute of Archaeology of the Hebrew University of Jerusalem.

The Destruction Caused by Drainage Activities along the Jordan River

Between September and December 1999 highly destructive drainage activities took place north and south of the bridges, including the study area. These activities caused serious damage to the Benot Ya'akov Formation both in the river bed and on its banks (Sharon et al., in press). The

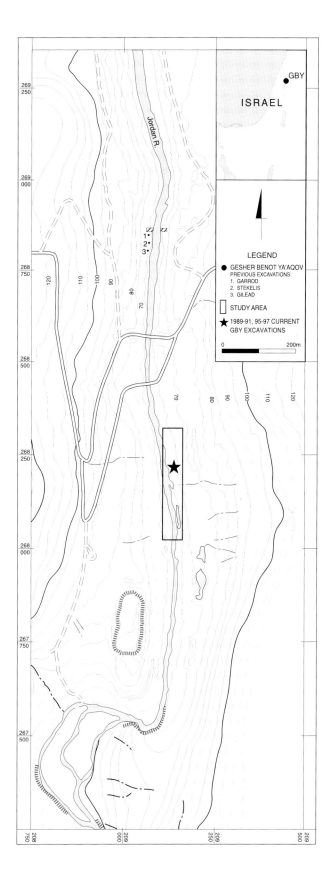

Figure 2: Location map of the Gesher Benot Ya'aqov site and vicinity.

Photo 10: A wood fragment quarried from the river bed (Sept.–Dec. 1999), Benot Ya'akov Formation (sector 39 of the Kinneret Drainage Authority).

works, intended to deepen the river bed, included the removal of basalt flows and the quarried material was dumped east of the Jordan River. Many wood fragments were observed along some 2.5 km of the Acheulian site, verifying earlier observations (described below) of the existence of wood north of the bridges (Photo 10). In addition to the destruction of the Acheulian strata, waterlogged Mousterian and Epi-Palaeolithic sites were destroyed. The deposits of all cultural entities comprised lithic, palaeontological and palaeobotanical assemblages. None of the wood fragments that originated in the drainage activities were conserved or anatomically examined.

Geology

The Acheulian site of GBY is stratified within the Benot Ya'akov Formation (Horowitz, 1979). These lacustrine and lake-margin sediments, along with the associated lower Pleistocene basalt flows, have been affected by tectonic activity along the north-south trending structural line known as the Jordan Lineament. Folding and faulting of these units have resulted in the formation of a narrow morphotectonic embayment located along a plate border (the Benot Ya'aqov Embayment) in the south-eastern part of the Hula Valley Basin (Belitzky, 1987; in press).

The deposits of the Benot Ya'akov Formation are the remains of a freshwater lake system which existed in the Hula Valley. The limnic-fluvial sediments of the formation were deposited in the embayment as well as in the Hula Basin *sensu stricto*. Additional tectonic activity, including left-lateral movement on a north-north-east-trending structural line (Goren-Inbar and Belitzky, 1989), produced folding and faulting of these deposits. The present exposure of the Benot Ya'akov Formation sediments is due to recent tectonic activity which uplifted the GBY strata and to incision caused by erosional processes (including dredging of the Jordan River) (Belitzky, in press; n.d.; Horowitz, 1979). The Benot Ya'aqov Embayment is the only location where the Benot Ya'akov Formation is exposed (Goren-Inbar et al., 1992a). These exposed sediments total some 34 m in thickness and can be assigned to the Lower/ Middle Pleistocene (Goren-Inbar et al., 2000). Deposition in the study area took place on the southernmost margin of the palaeo-Lake Hula (Feibel et al., 1998; Goren-Inbar et al., 1992a).

History of Research at GBY

Archaeological surveys and excavations were carried out at GBY between 1935 and 1968 (Photo 11) by Garrod, (Goren-Inbar and Belitzky, 1989; Goren-Inbar in prep.), Stekelis (1960; Stekelis et al., 1937; 1938) and Gilead (1968;

Photo 11: Waterlogged sediment excavated and photo-graphed by M. Stekelis' expedition (courtesy: Israel Antiquities Authority).

1970). These excavations encountered many difficulties, among which the water-saturated deposits resulting from the proximity of the Jordan River were of prime concern. As this proximity appeared to explain the waterlogged nature of the sediments, the possibility that it resulted from another source was never discussed. The influence of a shallow Pleistocene lake, the palaeo-Lake Hula, that preceded the Jordan River in this region, and the waterlogged nature of its sediment, were mentioned but never explained. None of the early reports mentions the preservation of organic material in the Pleistocene deposits.

The first indication of the existence of waterlogged wood at the site of GBY (the area reported on is between the British bridge and the Turkish one, located north of the present study area) is documented in the archives of the Israel Antiquities Authority. A detailed description of the wood observed is given in a series of documents written by Yariv Shapira, a 'Trustee of Antiquity', who witnessed, during July and August 1952, the exposure of a layer bearing Acheulian artefacts (handaxes), large mammal bones, a hearth and many wood fragments. All these were bedded in a layer 1.0–2.5 m thick that was exposed by quarrying an artificial channel for the Jordan River as part of the Hula Drainage Project. In a document written on 14 August 1952 (Appendix 1) Mr. Shapira described a concentration of large bones (which he suggested should be assigned to a single animal) in association with two flint handaxes and a bone tool. According to his observation, some 194 cm north of the bones remnants of a hearth were observed, with burned sediments, charcoal and the remains of fossil wood. He further mentioned a concentration of wooden logs located 260 cm further north, bedded in different positions (vertical, horizontal and inclined). Additional concentrations were observed by Mr. Shapira some 180 cm south of the large bones (wood as well as hearth remains). According to his description, the occurrences mentioned in detail above were not sporadic finds but were a component of a much larger archaeological phenomenon which included other exposures of the same nature. In his report Mr. Shapira

further investigated the nature of the recovered wood; he measured the logs as 10–18 cm in diameter. In order to find out more about the origin of the wood remains he attempted to expose one of the logs and was surprised to discover that its tip was 'pointed' (the report includes a drawing of the item) and that it was horizontally bedded. He concluded that the log could not have broken naturally and considered the suggestion of one of the labourers that it could have been the result of beaver activity (though none are known to exist in the local fauna). Further on in his report, he rejected this idea on the basis of the association of the wood pieces with many other prehistoric remains, which supported his hypothesis that the wood found was a result of prehistoric human activities. The report continued by speculating about reasons for the accumulation of the wood, considering, for the first time, preservation due to anaerobic conditions. Regretfully, despite references to photographs attached to the original report, none exist at present in the archives.

High water levels limited visibility and hindered work during Stekelis' excavations. He noted that excavations could not take place without continuous pumping (Stekelis, 1960). The presence of abundant organic material was observed by the excavators only in the black patina on the flint artefacts.

The first published mention of wood remains at the GBY site was made by Bar-Yosef (1975: 589), where they were referred to as 'fossil wood' which was observed north of the bridges in the sections of the Jordan River bank (personal observation by N. G.-I., early 1970s). This was followed by a preliminary report on the wood assemblage of GBY (Werker and Goren-Inbar, 2001).

Palaeobotanical Research at GBY

Palaeobotanical assemblages and isolated botanical remains predating the Neolithic period are rare discoveries in the Levant and in the Mediterranean climatic zone. This is typical of all regions of Israel and is a result of chemical, physical and biological weathering and destruction (Rowell and Barbour, 1990). The most common palaeobotanical finds are charcoal remains, which are more abundant in

Photo 12: Wood *in situ* in the Jordan River.

Photo 13: Wood *in situ* in the Jordan River.

Palaeolithic sites than in non-archaeological settings. However, the presence of charcoal in the most ancient deposits associated with hominin activities is minimal. The available Israeli palaeobotanical assemblages of wood usually derive from two distinctly different environments of deposition: extremely dry conditions (in desert and semi-desert regions) and wet sites (the anaerobic environments of waterlogged sediments). The former have yielded some of the most striking finds, such as the assemblages from Nahal Hemar Cave and those from the Cave of the Warrior (Bar-Yosef and Alon, 1988; Schick, 1998). Waterlogged occurrences include sites in the Mediterranean Sea (Hartman, 1997), as well as sites associated with freshwater bodies such as Ohalo II (Simchoni, 1998) in the Sea of Galilee and GBY, which presently partly underlies the Jordan River.

Previously unknown outcrops of the Benot Ya'akov Formation (Goren-Inbar and Belitzky, 1989) were identified, for example, on the eastern slopes of Metzad Ateret (also known as Le Chastellet or Vadum Jacob), a Crusader fortress located on the west bank of the river, south of the bridges. There, where the formation comprises the *glacis* of the fortress, a handaxe and the characteristic gastropod *Viviparus apameae* were identified (Goren-Inbar and Belitzky, 1989: fig. 2). However, these exposures are entirely devoid of signs of organic material. It was only during additional surveys, conducted closer to the bank of the Jordan River, that organic material was observed to be eroding from the sediments (Photos 12–14).

The palaeobotanical research potential of the site of GBY was first recognized when renewed surveys along the Jordan River banks took place (1981–1989) during work carried out in preparation for the renewal of excavations. Pieces of wood (the macrobotanical component as defined by Birks, 1980) were repeatedly observed eroding out of the left bank of the river. These were collected, catalogued, conserved and stored for future analysis. These wood segments varied greatly in size and shape, and they were and bark segments which are the subject of the present study, and yielded the contextual information about the wood (Figure 3).

The palaeobotanical assemblage originating in the archaeological excavations at GBY is only one of many multidisciplinary research topics currently undergoing investigation. The botanical research is divided into two fields: the woody remains (wood and bark) and other

Photo 14: The same wood out of the water (*Pistacia atlantica*)

anatomically identified as comprising both wood and bark. In order to verify their antiquity, a few pieces were sent for ^{14}C dating (Goren-Inbar and Belitzky, 1989; Goren-Inbar et al., 1992a). A single large item (*Pistacia atlantica*) was taken out of the water (Photo 14) and cut into several pieces which were then analysed in two different ^{14}C laboratories for age determination. The results yielded ages that are beyond the range of the technique (Goren-Inbar et al., 1992a), a confirmation of the wood's antiquity.

The value of the data collected on numerous field trips during this preliminary phase of the study became evident at a later stage when excavations were carried out (1989–1997) in the study area. This initial phase was of great importance in enabling us to accumulate experience and develop methodologies of registration, transportation and conservation of this fragile class of finds so rare in the Levant.

Seven field seasons of excavations (1989–1997) at GBY resulted in the exposure and recovery of the many wood

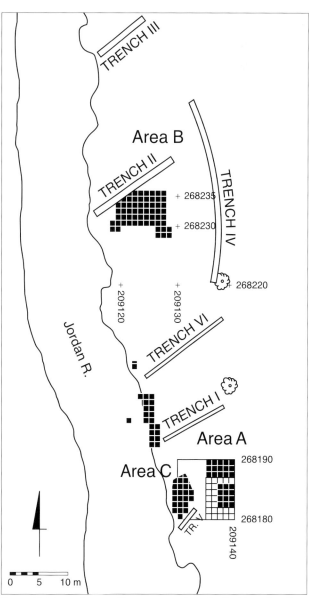

Figure 3: Map of excavation areas and geological trenches in the study area.

evidence (fruits, seeds, phytoliths and pollen). Though the preservation encountered at the site included other elements of the plant domain such as foliage and stems, their fragmentary condition did not enable detailed analysis and identification.

The early Quaternary flora of the Hula Valley area and its adjacent regions is known mainly from palynological evidence. Several cores have been analysed, mostly of Holocene and Upper Pleistocene age, demonstrating changes in plant cover and characterized by changing ratios of arboreal/non–arboreal pollen taxa (AP/NAP) (Baruch and Bottema, 1991; Horowitz, 1979). Most of these works assigned climatic interpretations to the observed record, attempting to establish a correlation with the European palaeoclimatic record. A few of the deeper cores yielded data from earlier strata, including the Benot Ya'akov Formation (Picard, 1952). Rarely, deeper levels were penetrated, (e.g. Emek Hula 1 and Notera 3; Horowitz, 1979, 1989). Four samples obtained from outcrops of the Benot Ya'akov Formation were analysed by Horowitz (1989: 222), yielding additional information about the plant cover of the Hula Valley and its environs in ancient times. This palynological evidence will be integrated with data derived from the site, which are currently undergoing investigation.

The present study concerns only the woody remains from the site. The remains of seeds and fruits are being studied by Y. Melamed of Bar-Ilan University, Israel. The preliminary analysis of this material (Melamed, 1997) demonstrates an outstanding wealth and excellent preservation of thousands of specimens. The study yielded a striking number of plant taxa identifications.

The purpose of this study of the wood segments from the GBY site is to obtain additional data that may differ from the palynological data. The segments are mostly waterlogged and therefore represent events that occurred in close geographical proximity to the site, in contrast to the long-distance transport potential of airborne pollen. The research potential of the wood segments has definitely not been exhausted; future studies will be concerned with striations, usage, genetics and others. This study, however, contributes some understanding of one aspect of the palaeoenvironment of the Hula Valley during Lower/Middle Pleistocene times. This particular subject has been chosen to initiate the sequence of reports which all aim at achieving a better understanding of the palaeoenvironment in the Hula Valley during this period. The palaeoenvironment and specifically the vegetation in this part of the Levant are key issues for the understanding of both animal and hominin behaviour.

Chapter 2 – Methodology

The wood assemblage reported on here was collected from a variety of contexts during the reconnaissance and excavation stages of the project between 1989 and 1997. Though some material was recovered from natural exposure along the Jordan River banks, most was excavated from the site. Different approaches to the excavation of the archaeological surfaces and the geological trenches resulted in differences in the precision of attribution of the wood pieces, as well as in their conservation. The wood was also found in several different stratigraphic settings, both primary and derived, which complicated their attribution. The methods employed in the collection, initial conservation and examination of the wood pieces are detailed below.

Location and Stratigraphic Assignment of the GBY Wood

The wood segments were encountered in four different contexts:

1) Eroding from sediments (the Benot Ya'akov Formation) underlying the Jordan River or in its banks. The amount of the erosion is determined by the changing velocity of the river and by the fluctuating water level, which is artificially controlled upstream.

2) In the Holocene floodplain deposits of the Jordan River.

3) In Early/Middle Pleistocene deposits that were mechanically quarried out of the geological trenches, deposited on the banks of the trench and then manually searched for the presence of wood segments, stone artefacts and fossil bones.

4) In the archaeological horizons, excavated from *in situ* contexts within a gridded area.

While the collections discussed here consist primarily of *in situ* materials, some useful information could be gleaned from the other wood pieces.

Wood segments lacking detailed stratigraphic assignment

The first three categories listed above include wood segments that cannot be assigned securely to a particular stratum. In some cases assignment would have been possible within a limited range, but all are considered here as not being *in situ*. Despite this, it is evident that they are not Recent specimens. In most cases (especially those in category 1) sediment and molluscs of the Benot Ya'akov Formation adhered to the segments (Photos 15–18). The floodplain material category (item 2) was divided into two subcategories. The first includes wood segments that were found stratigraphically at the base of this unit. They were associated with many stone artefacts and bones that eroded from the tilted beds of the Benot Ya'akov Formation and were later deposited horizontally and unconformably on top of the *in situ* Benot Ya'akov Formation strata (that is, they lie at the unconformity). Most of the wood remains originating from this stratigraphical position in Areas A, B (Layer II-1) and C (Layer V-1) were discarded due to their insecure stratigraphic position, though a small sample was

14

0 ▬▬▬▬▬ 2 cm

Photo 15: Bark segment found eroding from the Jordan River bank.

0 ▬▬▬▬▬ 2 cm

Photo 16: Bark segment found eroding from the Jordan River bank.

Photo 17: Wood segment found embedded in the Jordan River bank.

0 ▬▬▬▬▬ 5 cm

retained for control purposes and will be dealt with in the following chapters. The second subcategory includes unidentified organic material that was bedded within the floodplain deposit (mainly in sands). This material was discarded except for three samples that were analysed by AMS ^{14}C in order to obtain the date of the deposit. These yielded Holocene ages (R. Housely, pers. com. 1994).

The third context includes all wood segments that originated from the mechanical excavation (by backhoe) of six trenches which were quarried for structural, stratigraphical and sedimentological purposes in the study area (Figure 3). Both faces of these trenches were cleaned, and some wood pieces became visible while still *in situ*. Other pieces were collected from the sediment heaps (*déblai*) resulting from these trenching activities. Waterlogged wood pieces like the latter were collected immediately upon discovery, as any delay caused rapid shrinkage and hence distortion of the wood structure as a result of desiccation. This source yielded most of the items that could not be assigned to a specific archaeological horizon, layer or level. Despite this, they were most informative as to the presence of the organic component in the stratigraphical sequence.

Wood segments with detailed stratigraphic assignment

All segments of wood encountered in the archaeological

excavations were plotted in three dimensions, and detailed information on their stratigraphic and sedimentologic context is available. Though the documentation of this *in situ* material follows standard conventions, the complexities of the stratigraphic setting at GBY required a more elaborate spatial frame of reference.

A grid, aligned with the Israel Grid, was applied to the study area to serve as a reference system for the spatial locations of finds originating in the excavation. A steel cable grid of one-metre squares was suspended over the area intended for excavation. The archaeological horizons, however, have been tilted by tectonic forces, and thus excavation along the strike and dip of the layer (Figure 4) resulted in an inclined surface. Consequently, the excavated surface in each square marked by the grid is not a true square, but the projection of a square on a sloping surface (Figure 5), resulting in a surface exposure larger than 1 m^2. The surface excavated is determined by two angles: that of the strike (i.e. the angle at which it transects the grid) and that of the horizon's dip. Once the artefact-bearing horizons were laterally exposed, the finds were mapped, photographed, and their exact position recorded before removal.

Mapping and drafting were carried out continuously during excavation. Most maps were drawn at a scale of 1:5 on Mylar sheets to minimize distortion. The items were mapped as if viewed perpendicularly to the horizon and

Photo 18: Wood segment found embedded in the Jordan River bank.   0 ▬▬▬▬ 5 cm

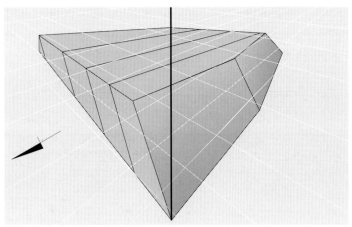

Figure 4: Grid system (excavation along strike and dip of the archaeological horizons).

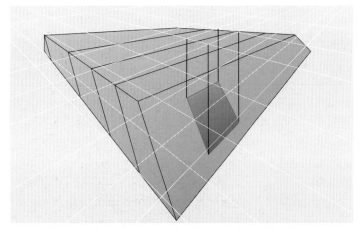

Figure 5: Size of excavated unit (projection of 1 m²).

this view is therefore not aligned with the grid (Figure 6). Correlation between the grid and the maps was made possible by marking the contact points of the grid's plumb lines on the drawings of the tilted horizons.

As described above, the standard unit of excavation was the projection of a 1 m square on a tilted surface. Each unit was further subdivided into four quadrants or subsquares. Excavation was carried out in each subsquare to an average depth of 5 cm. On exposure of a 'surface' (a scatter of finds) the process was halted and documentation by drawing and photography was carried out before removal of the finds. Coordinates were taken for all items larger than 2 cm, and each was also drawn on the maps.

Utilizing elevation controls (benchmarks) established with the site grid, elevations above msl were determined for the various surfaces and for the excavated items, using a combination of surveying instruments and line levels. At the beginning of each phase of excavation, the exact elevation of the subsquare to be excavated was registered, with readings taken at two opposite points, the highest (on the north-east) and the lowest (on the south-west). This procedure was carried out in order to record the tilt of the layers.

Pieces of wood were excavated using a variety of tools and methods. In coarse-grained sediments wood was exposed with ice picks and dental tools and with the constant application of brushes. In finer-grained sediments water was applied as an excavation tool, though frequently dental tools were also used. It should be noted that the GBY sediments are characterized by the presence of mollusc-bearing layers (coquina) and in Area B Layer II-6 also by fine-grained conglomerate, precluding a single excavation method using only very fine tools. The presence of hard materials in the soft deposit dictated the application of alternative methods in accordance with the sediment type.

Of the organic material, only pieces of wood longer than 2 cm were documented (drawn, coordinated and sometimes photographed). Other organic items were usually not visible during excavation and were detected only after they were wet-sieved in the laboratory. On exposure of an archaeological surface, the finds, especially the basalt artefacts and the pieces of wood, were watered constantly to prevent deformation due to shrinkage of the wood, and exfoliation and destruction of some of the basalt artefacts.

Registration, Storage and Transportation

The wood samples were placed after removal in plastic bags filled with water to prevent desiccation. Descriptive data for each wooden piece (location, size, layer, etc.) were written on Mylar with Mylar pencil and were kept in the water with the wood. The descriptive data were recorded on special forms when wood cleaning took place in the

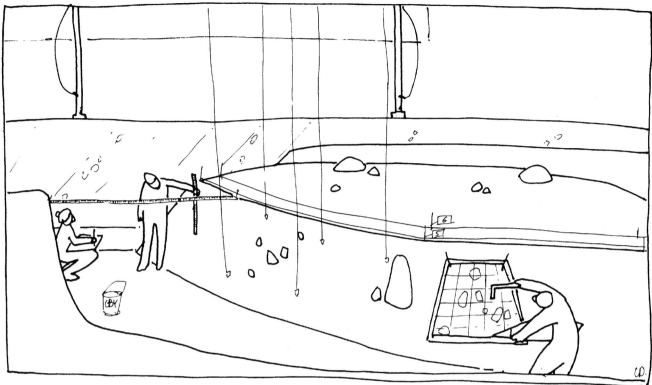

Figure 6: Mapping of the archaeological unit and its relation to the grid.

laboratory. Tags bearing the serial catalogue number for each segment or group of segments were inserted in the bags.

The longest wood pieces had to be treated differently in the field since their transportation in water proved destructive, causing many fractures and splitting of the brittle pieces. The procedure for their packing included placing each piece (after moistening) inside a long plastic sleeve together with a plastic irrigation pipe tilted upwards and the serial catalogue number. The top of the sleeve and the pipe were closed together with masking tape and placed inside a long cardboard box (Photos 19–20). Following this, Styrofoam was sprayed on one face of the sleeve. After drying the package was turned over and the same procedure took place on the other side. A catalogue number was inserted into the foam. After drying the package was ready for transportation and needed watering (through the pipe) only every few days.

Both types of wood pieces, those immersed in water in plastic bags and those cocooned in Styrofoam, were kept untouched until anatomically sampled and ready for the beginning of the conservation treatment.

Conservation
(based on a report by O. Cohen)

The several hundred pieces of wood found in the excavations varied in size from a few centimetres to over a metre in length. Pressure due to compaction and geological movements in the area had left stones and shells embedded in some of the wood surfaces and scratches on others. Some samples were very hard and it was difficult to insert a pin, though most were very soft and fragile.

Replicas of some of the large samples were made to allow studies of the surface details before conservation. The moulds were made of a thin silicon layer (Rhodorsil

Photo 19: Wood and plastic pipe in plastic sleeve.

Photo 20: Wood cocooned in Styrofoam.

RTV 573 by Rhône-Poulenc) supported by gypsum. The cast was of polyester resin with colouring pigments, reinforced with fibreglass cloth.

Since conservation started before full identification of all the woods, the treatment had to address a wide range of wood types in different states of preservation. An improvized laboratory was arranged for treating this large quantity of waterlogged wood. The excavated wood was kept in a plastic container with fresh water. By the time it reached the laboratory an odour indicating bacterial activity was discerned. The wood was cleaned of mud and treated with the biocide Kathon, 2–12 ppm in water (13.9 active agent produced by Rohm and Haas) (Dawson 1981; Cohen 1999). The conservation treatment was based on immersion in polyethylene glycol (PEG) in two stages (Hoffman, 1986). In the first stage PEG-400 (average molecular weight 400) was used for 8–12 months up to 50% concentration at room temperature. The second stage

followed with PEG-4000 up to 80% concentration at a temperature of 40–60°C. The period of immersion in the PEG-4000 was between one and two years according to the size of the treated segment. At the end of the process the wood was slowly dried out in a controlled environment to 60% relative humidity. As a result of the conservation treatment, the wood retained its appearance with all surface details. No deformation occurred and the shrinkage is between 0–4% at most. Considering the swelling typical of waterlogged wood, this is a satisfactory result.

Methods of Wood Preparation for Anatomical Examination

Wood anatomy is specific to the plant taxon, which may be a species, genus, subtribe or family. This enables identification of plants by microscopic examination of the anatomical characteristics of their wood. This knowledge is often applied as a tool in fields like archaeology and forensics. Identification of the GBY wood was carried out at the Anatomy Section of the Department of Botany, the Hebrew University of Jerusalem.

All wood segments studied were sampled prior to the conservation treatment. The wet segments of wood were sectioned by hand with a razor blade in cross, longitudinal radial, and longitudinal tangential directions. The sections were kept in a solution of water and glycerin (1:1) and examined under the light microscope. When necessary the sections were cleared with a solution of 4% NaOH.

The anatomical features of the wood segments were compared with slides of contemporary wood and with wood catalogues (Fahn et al., 1986; Greguss, 1955; 1959; Schweingruber, 1990).

A preliminary method for evaluating the extent of preservation of the organic material in the field was introduced through the use of a portable FTIR spectrometer in the 1991 field season (Weiner et al., 1995). Small wood samples were extracted from wood segments exposed during the excavation. Their analyses, which were conducted by Professor S. Weiner, demonstrated that the preservation of the different pieces was not uniform. Furthermore, some fragments included a secondary deposit of aragonite. This method proved useful but was not available during subsequent field seasons.

Chapter 3 – Geology

Introduction

The unique nature of the GBY wood assemblage is closely intertwined with aspects of its geological context. The accumulation and preservation of the wood resulted from geological circumstances in which tectonic subsidence facilitated burial on the margins of the palaeo-Lake Hula. Subsequent groundwater conditions protected the wood from destruction by aerobic processes. The stratigraphic sequence at the site records details of the changing environmental conditions in which the ancient woods were formed, transported, accumulated and buried. This sequence also preserves other geological records, such as the pattern of the Earth's magnetic field over time by which the site can be precisely dated. In addition, patterns in the sedimentary record reflect ancient climatic cycles from which the duration of deposition can be estimated, and correlation to global climatic cycles can be attempted. A detailed characterization of the sedimentary layers at the site thus provides insights into the history of accumulation of the GBY wood assemblage, as well as the setting for hominin occupation along this ancient shoreline.

Stratigraphy

The sedimentary strata exposed in the vicinity of the GBY archaeological site have been assigned to the Benot Ya'akov Formation based on the presence of the guide fossil *Viviparus apameae* (Horowitz, 1973). These comprise the only known surface exposures of this formation, which was defined from the Emek Hula 1 borehole. The type section of the formation in that borehole is 185 m thick

and consists of calcareous mudstone rich in molluscs, with several organic-rich levels. In the Emek Hula 1 borehole, the Benot Ya'akov Formation overlies the Ayyelet HaShahar Formation (organic-rich carbonates and peat), and is conformably overlain by the Hulata Formation (the 'Main Peat'). Studies along the banks of the Jordan River have shown that the sedimentary strata of the Benot Ya'akov Formation there overlie a basalt, thought to correlate with the Yarda Basalt, with an age of 0.9 ± 0.15 Ma (Goren-Inbar, 1992). The outcrops along the Jordan River do not expose stratigraphic contacts with the under- or overlying sedimentary formations, and the Benot Ya'akov strata are unconformably overlain by more recent deposits of the Jordan River floodplain. The Ashmura Formation, which conformably overlies the Hulata Formation in the subsurface of the Hula Basin, does crop out in the vicinity of the site (especially to the north-east), but is not seen in direct relationship with the Benot Ya'akov deposits.

Benot Ya'akov strata are strongly tilted and folded in their exposures along the river, due to their proximity to the Jordan Fault Line (Belitzky, in press). The strata strike roughly north-west and dip 15–45° to the south-west (Figure 7). This attitude, coupled with the alternating resistant and non-resistant character of the lithologies, is reflected in the character of the eastern bank of the Jordan River, which is marked by a pattern of alternating promontories and bays.

Investigations of the Benot Ya'akov Formation at GBY within the present study included examination of outcrops along the banks of the Jordan River, surfaces exposed in

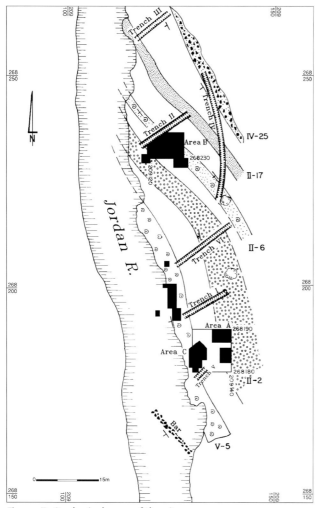

Figure 7: Geological map of the site.

the archaeological work, and the excavation of six geological trenches (Trenches I–VI) by backhoe. These trenches were sited primarily to provide an overlapping sequential profile through the local Benot Ya'akov strata (although Trench IV was excavated in an attempt to slow groundwater flow into the archaeological excavation). Each of the trenches was profiled and sampled, and the data allowed construction of lithologic columns for each trench (Figure 8), which was compiled into a composite for the site. There is significant local variation in the facies exposed in the trenches, but the persistence of prominent marker beds, and tracing of beds between the trenches, permitted secure correlation.

In the local stratigraphic sequence, Benot Ya'akov Formation strata attain a thickness of a little over 34 m (Figure 9). A wide range of lithologies is represented, ranging from boulder conglomerates to fine-grained carbonates and coquinas. Individual strata may vary considerably in thickness laterally, and some are seen to pinch out even within the relatively restricted spatial perspective of the study area.

The stratigraphic sequence can be interpreted as reflecting two types of sedimentary cycles. A first-order cycle is seen through the entire sequence in the major facies shift from fluvial conglomerates at the base to lacustrine muds and coquinas through the bulk of the

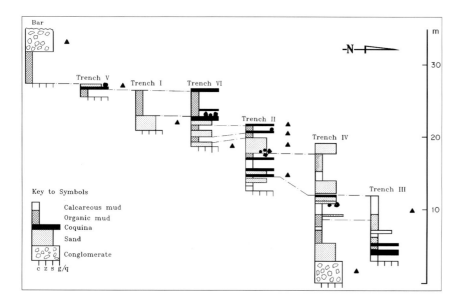

Figure 8: Stratigraphic columns from the geological trenches.

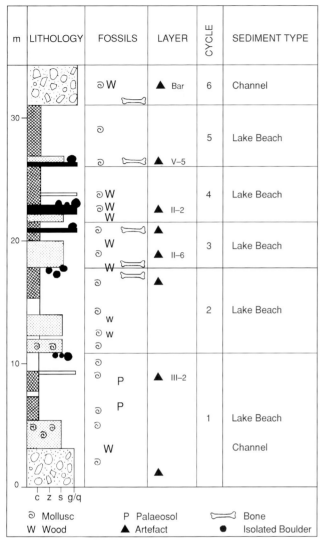

Figure 9: Composite section of Benot Ya'akov Formation strata at the site.

Many of the sands and coquinas which represent beach facies are interpreted as reflecting one or more storm events (Feibel, 2001). These shoreface accretionary units are particularly well represented in Layer II-6, and were responsible for the burial of much of the wood there.

The wood assemblage discussed in this volume derives from Cycles 2, 3, 4 and 5 of the composite section (Figure 9). Wood specimens were also recorded from Cycle 1, at the top of the basal conglomerate, and from Cycle 6 at the 'Bar' (Goren-Inbar et al., 1992b), but none were adequately preserved for inclusion in this study. The wood specimens were attributed to two variants of stratigraphic context: those from *within* a stratigraphic layer and those from *between* stratigraphic layers (Table 4). This has important implications for the taphonomy and depositional history of the wood.

Table 4: Stratigraphic and sedimentological context of the wood segments.

Layer	Contact	Wood Specimens	Lithology	% OC
V-5		7	molluscan packstone	3.5
	V-5/6	14		
V-6		7	calcareous mud	
I-4		13	calcareous mud	
	I-4/5	3		
I-5		13	molluscan packstone	
II-2		67	molluscan packstone	1.5
	II-2/3	14		
	II-3/4	4		
II-4		5	gravel	2.5
	II-4/5	2		
II-5		39	molluscan wackestone	9.5
	II-5/6	13		
VI-14		18	molluscan packstone	
II-6 L 1		144	molluscan packstone	
II-6 L 2		78	molluscan packstone	
II-6 L 3		24	molluscan packstone	
II-6 L 4		46	molluscan packstone	
II-6 L 5		5	molluscan packstone	2
II-6 L 6		3	molluscan packstone	
II-6 L 7		99	molluscan packstone	
	II-6/7	11		
II-7		23	calcareous mud	13
	II-7/8	6		
II-12		1	molluscan packstone	4.5
II-14		3	molluscan packstone	6
TOTAL		662		
AVG		25		

section, and back to conglomerates at the top. Within this first-order cycle are nested five second-order cycles (Cycles 1–5 of Figure 9) that reflect changes within the lacustrine facies. These are marked by a shift from coarser-grained lithologies, mostly coquinas and sands, to fine-grained muds, reflecting a deepening trend at the lake margin.

Beyond the cyclicity apparent in the stratigraphic pattern, numerous shorter-term 'events' are reflected in individual depositional units and in post-depositional modification. Soil structure is apparent at two levels within Cycle 1, and can be seen in both Trench III and Trench IV.

Sedimentology

Benot Ya'akov Formation sediments preserved at GBY reflect a variety of lake-margin depositional settings, including alluvial channels bringing boulders and gravel to the lake edge, shoreface molluscan packstones and sands, and lacustrine muds. The sequence is highly calcareous (individual units up to 91% $CaCO_3$), and most layers are carbonaceous to some extent (generally 2–12% but up to 41% organic C).

The sediments can be grouped broadly into four lithofacies, interpreted as representing different depositional environments along an ancient lake margin. The boulder to cobble conglomerates, which are clast-supported and have a matrix of sandy molluscan hash, represent alluvial channels verging on the lake margin. They are most prominent at the base and top of the study interval, but more restricted lenticular gravels occur at the bases of Cycles 2 and 3. Molluscan packstones and sands are indicative of beach deposition. These strata commonly occur as 10–20 cm beds, many of which may reflect storm-generated beachface accretion (Feibel, 2001). The size, sorting and degree of breakage among the molluscs reflects the duration of exposure on the beach, as well as minor reworking by waves. The calcareous muds are visually divisible into two types, one that is nearly black and the other commonly a grey-brown colour. The black muds typically have 5% or more organic carbon, while the grey-brown muds have 2% or less. These appear to reflect two offshore settings in which fine-grained biochemical carbonate was accumulating, one in which circulation was poor and organic supply high, and a second in which circulation was better and fewer organics were deposited. These may represent offshore locations where standing vegetation occurred, versus those where open-water conditions prevailed.

Wood was encountered in over 25 stratigraphic levels at the site. The wood specimens were found in a wide range of lithologies, from molluscan packstones (e.g. Layer II-2) to calcareous muds (e.g. Layer II-7). Those specimens that were recovered from layer contacts occurred in two situations. Some were sandwiched between two layers of

molluscan packstone, while others were preserved between a molluscan packstone and a calcareous mud. The consistent association of the wood with packstones, interpreted as representing beach accumulations, supports the hypothesis of driftwood accumulation discussed in Chapter 5.

Preservation of the GBY wood was dependent upon the maintenance of anoxic conditions. These conditions persisted from shortly after burial of the wood until excavation. In addition to the evidence of the wood itself, several lines of evidence demonstrate the anoxic character of the sediments. Gley colours were encountered in many layers immediately upon excavation. These low chroma blue-green hues often faded within hours of excavation. The presence of fine-grained pyrite in organic-rich muds, along with examples of pyrite infillings in mammalian long bones, also demonstrates the anoxic character of these muds through time.

Chronology

The age of the GBY wood assemblages discussed here is of particular significance for two reasons. The site is of great antiquity, at 780 Ka, astride the Lower/Middle Pleistocene boundary. This places the site in a temporal window that is poorly sampled from other sites and regions. It is of considerable interest for a wide range of questions, ranging from aspects of environmental change and climatic effects within the last Ice Age to details of the context of hominin migrations out of Africa. Our ability to pinpoint the age of the site precisely makes it a reference datum. Records from temporally uncontrolled sites, including the evolutionary patterns of plants and animals and the technological record of stone tool production, can be calibrated by the controlled record and sequence at GBY.

Early recognition of the Acheulian character of stone tools from GBY, along with the affinities of the fossil faunas associated with them, had long placed the site in the relative framework of the Middle Pleistocene. This attribution was supported by isotopic ages on the Yarda Basalt, located stratigraphically beneath the site, but allowed only rough approximation of the numerical age of GBY to about 500 Ka (Goren-Inbar et al., 1992a).

During the 1997 field season, sampling was undertaken for a detailed magnetostratigraphic study based on the exposures in the geological trenches. A suite of 155 oriented sediment samples, collected in plastic boxes, was analysed in the laboratory of Dr. Kenneth Verosub at the University of California at Davis (Goren-Inbar et al., 2000). These samples established a magnetostratigraphy for 26 m of the composite section. In the local magnetic polarity stratigraphy, a reversed magnetozone is recorded from the lower 9 m of the sampled interval, and a normal magnetozone is documented in the overlying 17 m sampled interval. The only reasonable correlation of the reversed-to-normal polarity transition with the geomagnetic polarity timescale, taking into account the associated archaeological and palaeontological evidence, along with the age on the Yarda Basalt, is with the Matuyama-Brunhes Chron boundary, dated to 780 Ka (Bassinot et al., 1994). This coincides with Oxygen Isotope Stage 19.

The magnetostratigraphic evidence provides a single timeline close to the boundary between the first and second sedimentary cycles within the lacustrine portion of the sequence (Figure 9). The character of the cyclicity of the stratigraphic sequence permits an interpretation of the duration of deposition for the composite section, and thus development of an age model for the entire GBY section. The pattern of five second-order cycles nested within a single first-order cycle suggests that these may reflect Milankovitch periodicities of precession and eccentricity, at roughly 20 Ka and 100 Ka respectively. Applying this interpretation to the magnetostratigraphically-calibrated section at GBY suggests that the base of the composite section has an age of roughly 800 Ka, while the top of the section would date to 700 Ka. A 100 Ka period of deposition for the sequence is supported by detailed analysis of the magnetic properties of the sediments (Goren-Inbar et al., 2000), and is reasonable given the character of the deposits themselves.

Chapter 4 – Wood Identification and Plant Communities

> 'In the earliest historical period of the country, the days of the patriarchs,… the primeval forest still covered the hills, affording covert to the wild beasts and modifying the temperature of the air.'
>
> (Tristram, 1887: 6)
>
> '… It is covered with low, scattered oaks….. the oaks on our road ceased, except here and there a few; but they extended far to the East, on the plain at the base of Hermon.'
>
> (Forest, 1894: 240)

Introduction

The wood samples found at GBY were waterlogged, and many were soft and brittle. They were found to be in various stages of preservation. Nevertheless, in all of them the cell walls consisted of organic material, though it was sometimes partly degraded. Therefore, the segments were botanically not fossilized. As reported in Chapter 2, however, some fragments included a secondary deposit of aragonite.

The main anatomical features of wood that aid in plant identification are the arrangement, size and structure of the different types of cells which comprise the wood. Some of these features are conservative, while others are more variable. Small differences in features may sometimes lead to different identifications. On the other hand, intraspecific variations should also be taken into consideration. A list of the anatomical characteristics that could be observed for each of the identified taxa is given in this chapter.

In order to learn as much as possible about the vegetation during the Pleistocene, the present-day habitats of the identified plant species, as well as the ancient plant communities, are described and compared.

Wood Identification

The wood sample originating from the GBY excavations consists of all the segments longer than 2 cm which were recovered during the seven field seasons (1989–1997). The segments were catalogued and conserved as described in Chapter 2. Table 5 presents the inventory of wood segments and the number of identified and unidentified segments. The total number of segments counted during the sampling procedure for wood anatomy analysis was higher than that encountered during excavation and initial cataloguing. This difference resulted from fragmentation caused by fissures and breaks, both visible (Photo 21) and invisible during exposure. The fissured or broken segments had been 'glued' together to form a single item by fine clays and silts, which were washed away when the wood was immersed in water for storage and conservation purposes. Many pieces which were too small for anatomical hand sectioning were not kept.

A substantial number of wood fragments were conjoined either in the preliminary registration phase or during the anatomical sampling phase. Of the total of 1403 segments available after conjoining, 916 wood specimens

Table 5: Numbers of wood segments excavated and those botanically analysed.

Type of segment	N
Segments recovered at GBY excavations	1568
Segments after conjoining	1403
Segments botanically examined	916
Segments botanically identified as wood	638
Segments botanically identified as bark	97
Segments botanically unidentifiable	181

Photo 21: Fissured and broken wood segment *in situ*.

were sectioned and anatomically examined. Only 181 wood segments could not be identified (bark not included) for any of the following reasons:

a. Desiccation of the waterlogged wood before sectioning, either after excavation due to unfavourable preservation conditions or at some period in the past before excavation. Desiccation results in a change in dimensions by shrinkage of the cell walls and by folding over of the cell walls against each other, and sometimes also by the shrinkage of the amorphous chemicals that often fill the cells' lumen (Florian, 1990; Gale and Cutler, 2000). Twisting can occur as well. The extent to which the desiccated pieces of wood shrank and became distorted, sometimes beyond recognition, varied in accordance with their anatomical features. Wood with thin cell walls, for example, is more liable to shrinkage, while different cellulose direction of the microfibrils in different cells and/or cell wall layers may be responsible for twisting.

b. Differences in the extent of wood preservation between species may result from the wood's response to other external physical conditions such as pressure, which may also cause shrinkage and distortion. The extent of damage depends on the wood structure, cell wall thickness and chemical consistency of the walls, and lumen of the cells. Such shrinkage effects are seen, for instance, in the wood of *Salix*, which consists of thin-walled fibres and numerous, relatively thin-walled vessels. Its wood, therefore, easily becomes compressed under pressure or shrinks after drying (Plate 21B). The wood of *Ficus carica* contains tangential bands of thin-walled parenchyma cells which alternate with thick-walled fibres. In the three identified samples of this species the parenchyma bands are highly compressed and the fibres appear almost amalgamated (Plate 6). *Pistacia*, on the other hand, is relatively well preserved due to its thick-walled fibres, tyloses in vessels, prominent spiral thickenings on the vessel walls (Plate 1) and cell lumina filled with dark materials in the heartwood.

c. Wood degradation by biotic or chemical agents. The wood at the GBY site was immersed in water and buried in sediments. These are anoxic or almost anoxic conditions. Under such conditions 'bacterial erosion appears to be the main form of degradation in buried archaeological woods' rather than fungi (Kim and Singh, 2000:144). Fungi had superficially infected some of the wood segments. As has been suggested by Sakai (Sakai, 1991, cited by Kim and Singh, 2000) for buried wood in Japan, the wood '… must have been attacked by fungi under aerobic conditions prior to their burial' (Kim and Singh, 2000, citing Sakai, 1991). Differential chemical degradation of cell wall materials may also occur. In waterlogged wood there is excessive swelling of the cell walls followed by loosening of the secondary cell wall as a result of the hydrolysis of carbohydrates; subsequently collapse of the lignin skeleton occurs (Hoffman and Jones, 1990).

d. In some specimens, roots of contemporary plants have penetrated into the soft waterlogged wood, somewhat obliterating its structure (Plate 21C).

In all the above cases, gross anatomical structure or more delicate details like fine spiral thickenings, the type of pits or the presence of crystals may be hard to distinguish. Identification, therefore, may become impossible or uncertain.

e. Some of the specimens were young branches with very few growth rings. The wood structure in the first growth rings may be different from that of more mature wood and therefore less characteristic.

f. In ring-porous wood, narrow growth rings consisting mainly of large vessels of the earlywood are often produced during years of drought or under other types of stress. If the section includes only such rings the wood may appear diffuse-porous. The wood may therefore be mistakenly identified unless a wider growth ring with latewood narrow vessels can also be distinguished in the section (Plate 8A–C).

g. Wood samples were naturally taken for anatomical examination from the margins of the segments, where all the processes of damage due to the various causes mentioned above, including mechanical friction, are usually the greatest.

h. The wood of 13 anatomically identical segments, designated here as 'unknown tree', was fairly well preserved but we could not find wood of comparable anatomy, either in the printed literature or in the computerized data base (Wheeler et al., 1986) (see below).

Table 6 presents all unidentified pieces according to their stratigraphic level (trenches and layers). Many of these pieces derive from the quarrying activities of the geological trenches (I, II). The quarried deposit was dumped along the trenches, burying the wood fragments and thus delaying their recovery. This contributed to the desiccation process, and hence caused deformation of the pieces. The high proportion of unidentified pieces from Layer II-2 most probably stems from the fact that this coquina layer is

Table 6: Distribution of unidentifiable wood segments according to layers and interfaces.

Layer	N	%
Jordan River Bank	27	14.91
V–5	3	1.65
V–5/6	3	1.65
V–6	2	1.10
Trench I	6	3.31
I-4	8	4.41
I-4/5	4	2.20
I-5	5	2.76
Trench II	13	7.18
II–1	1	0.55
II–2	13	7.18
II–4	1	0.55
II–5	13	7.18
II–5/6	3	1.65
II–6	65	35.91
VI–14	4	2.20
II–6/7	2	1.10
II–7	3	1.65
II–12	2	1.10
Layer unknown	3	1.65
Total	181	99.89

extremely porous and lay close to the surface. Hence it was more likely to have been exposed to repeated periods of dry conditions, as opposed to deeper layers which were more continuously waterlogged. This rationale does not explain the similar value encountered for Layer II-5, which is a fine-grained black mud. The highest total number of segments recovered is that encountered in Layer II-6, which is further subdivided by level. Accordingly, the number of unidentified segments here is high as well. As seen in Table 7, the distribution of identified and

Table 7: Distribution of identified and unidentifiable wood segments in the levels of Layer II-6.

II-6 level	unidentifiable		identified	
	N	%	N	%
1	29	42.03	142	39.55
2	10	14.49	68	18.94
3	3	4.35	21	5.85
4	5	7.25	41	11.42
5	1	1.45	4	1.11
6	0	0	3	0.83
7	21	30.43	80	22.28
Total	69	100.0	359	99.98

unidentified wood fragments is very similar in each of the levels of Layer II-6. This could suggest a systematic loss of one or more woody taxa that are more prone to degradation, or more likely may relate to a longer interval of exposure of these levels on the lake shore prior to burial.

Tables 8–14 are presentations of the analysis of wood identifications according to different classifications. Included are taxa frequencies (Table 8), taxa distribution in layers of Area C (Table 9), in Trench I and layers of Area A (Table 10), in Trenches II, VI and Layer VI-14 of Area B (Table 11), in layers of Trench II (Table 12), in the levels of Layer II-6 (Table 13), and a detailed presentation of taxa frequencies in all layers and levels (Table 14).

Anatomical Characteristics of Wood of the Examined Species

The methods of wood preparation for anatomical examination are described in Chapter 2. The main anatomical characteristics of the wood, which aided in plant identification, are described here (anatomical features which could not be discerned in the sectioned material due to its poor preservation are not described).

Anacardiaceae

Pistacia: Vessels mostly in multiples and clusters. Walls of vessels, except for the widest, and of vascular tracheids with prominent spiral thickenings. Rays uni- and multiseriate, heterocellular, with short margins of square, upright, sometimes slightly procumbent cells and procumbent central cells. Gum ducts present in some of the multiseriate rays. In the three species described below solitary prismatic crystals are found in marginal ray cells.

Pistacia atlantica (Plate 1): Growth rings distinct. Wood ring- to semi-ring-porous, usually with one row of wide pores at the beginning of growth rings. Rays 1–5(6) cells wide, predominantly 4–5.

Pistacia vera: Growth rings distinct. Wood ring- to semi-ring-porous, usually with several rows of wide pores at the beginning of growth rings. Rays 1–5 cells wide, predominantly 3–4 (Grundwag and Werker, 1976).

Pistacia palaestina: Growth rings distinct. Wood ring-

porous with gradual decrease in pore diameter. Rays 1–4, predominantly 3 cells wide.

Rhus pentaphylla/tripartita (Plate 2): Growth rings faint. Vessels mainly in 2–7 radial multiples, some solitary, rounded in cross section, with thin-walled tyloses, spiral thickenings absent. Fibres mostly septate. Rays 1–3(4)-seriate, heterocellular, usually with 1–2 rows of square to upright marginal cells and procumbent to upright central cells.

Apocynaceae

Nerium: Growth rings faint. Vessels diffuse, solitary and in radial multiples, of a small diameter. Fibres thin-walled. In the examined specimen it is difficult to distinguish the vessels from the fibres. Rays 1–2(3) cells wide, heterocellular with low portions of strongly procumbent cells and tall margins of square to upright cells.

Araliaceae

Hedera: Vessels diffuse, mainly in clusters, sometimes in tangential or radial multiples of 2–4, occasionally solitary, often forming together with vasicentric tracheids a pattern of tangential bands. Vessel walls occasionally with spiral thickenings. Rays 1–7(14)-seriate, up to ca. 1.5 mm high, nearly homocellular to heterocellular, composed of procumbent central cells and slightly procumbent, square, and sometimes upright marginal cells.

Asclepiadaceae

Periploca: Vessels diffuse, mostly solitary, sometimes in pairs, sometimes in a radial or oblique pattern; of a small diameter. Fibres medium thick-walled. Rays mostly uniseriate, sometimes 2–3(4)-seriate up to 20 cells high; heterocellular composed of square, upright, sometimes weakly procumbent cells.

Caprifoliaceae

Lonicera: Growth rings distinct. Wood ring-porous (it is diffuse-porous in *Lonicera etrusca*, which grows today in the region, but ring-porous in other West Mediterranean species (Greguss, 1959; Schweingruber, 1990). Vessels

Table 8: Frequency of identified wood and unidentified bark.

Taxonomic identification	Common name	N	%
Amygdalus (korschinskii?)	Almond	1	0.15
Cedrus sp.	Cedar	2	0.29
Cerasus sp.	Cherry	1	0.15
Cerasus?		1	0.15
Crataegus sp.	Hawthorn	4	0.59
Ficus carica	Common fig	2	0.29
Ficus carica?		1	0.15
Fraxinus syriaca	Ash	245	36.08
Fraxinus?		28	4.12
Hedera sp.	Ivy	1	0.15
Jasminum sp.	Jasmine	1	0.15
Jasminum?		1	0.15
Juniperus sp.	Juniper	3	0.44
Lonicera sp.	Honeysuckle	5	0.75
Lonicera?		2	0.29
Lycium sp.	Box-thorn	1	0.15
Lycium?		3	0.44
Myrtus sp.	Myrtle	7	1.03
Myrtus?		2	0.29
Nerium?	Oleander	1	0.15
Olea europaea	Olive	45	6.63
Olea?		15	2.21
Periploca?	Silk-vine	1	0.15
Pistacia sp.	Pistachio	4	0.59
Pistacia?		3	0.44
Pistacia atlantica	Atlantic terebinth	25	3.68
Pistacia (atlantica?)		2	0.29
Pistacia atlantica/vera		8	1.18
Pistacia (palaestina?)	Palestine terebinth	1	0.15
Pistacia vera	Pistachio	3	0.44
Pistacia (vera?)		2	0.29
Populus sp.	Poplar	4	0.59
Populus?		1	0.15
Pyrus sp.	Pear	6	0.88
Pyrus?		2	0.29
Quercus calliprinos	Kermes oak	27	3.98
Quercus (calliprinos?)		3	0.44
Quercus ithaburensis		26	3.83
Quercus (ithaburensis?)		2	0.29
Quercus ithaburensis/calliprinos		11	1.62
Rhus pentaphylla/tripartita	Sumac	2	0.29
Rhus pentaphylla/tripartita?		1	0.15
Rhus?		1	0.15
Rosaceae, Prunoideae	Rose family	1	0.15
Salicaceae?	Willow family	2	0.29
Salix sp.	Willow	26	3.83
Salix?		8	1.18
Ulmus sp.	Elm	14	2.06
Vitis	Vine	2	0.29
Ziziphus/Paliurus	Jujube/Christ-thorn	2	0.29
unknown tree		13	1.91
bark	bark	97	14.28
bark?		7	1.03
Total		679	99.98

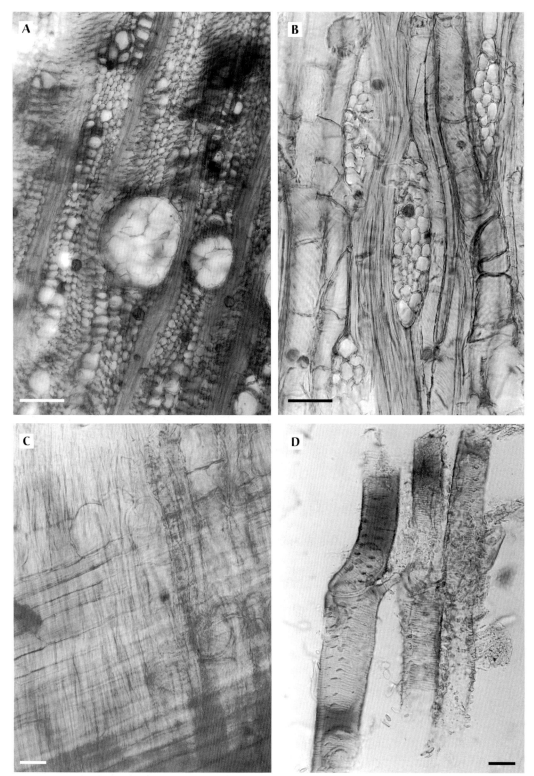

Plate 1: Wood specimens identified as *Pistacia atlantica*. A. Cross section. B. Tangential section. C. Radial section. D. Macerated vessel members with secondary spiral thickenings on their walls. Scale bars of A, B=100 μm; C, D=25 μm.

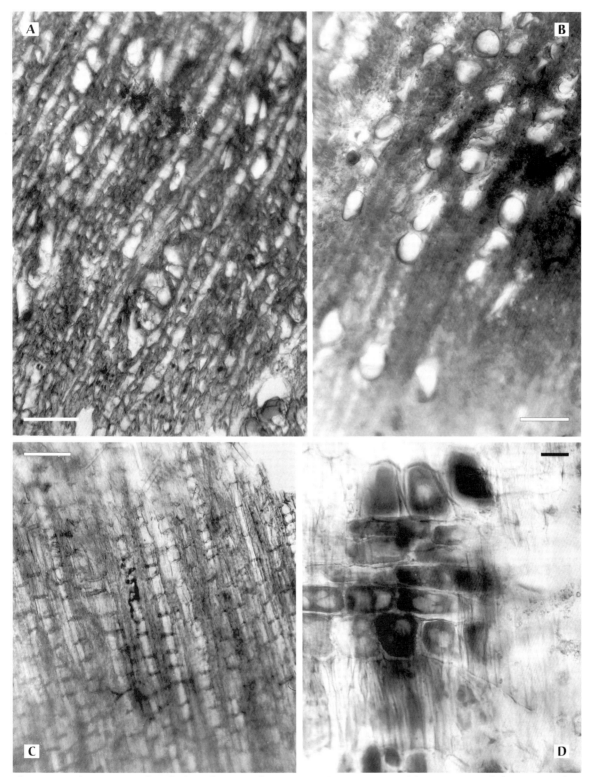

Plate 2: Wood specimens identified as *Rhus*. A and B. Cross sections. C. Tangential section. D. Radial section. Scale bars of A, B, C=100μm; D=25 μm.

generally solitary, rarely in small groups, angular in cross section; walls with fine spiral to annular thickenings. Rays 1–3(4)-seriate, of various heights up to more than 1 mm; heterocellular.

Cupressaceae

Juniperus (Plate 3): A gymnosperm, vascular elements consisting of tracheids only, with uniseriate bordered pits. Axial parenchyma diffuse or in short tangential bands. Rays mostly uniseriate, 1–8 cells high; pits 2–4 per cross-field. Resin ducts absent.

Fagaceae

Quercus: Vessels almost exclusively solitary, in a radial, flame-like or dendritic pattern. Vasicentric tracheids present. Parenchyma scanty paratracheal, and apotracheal diffuse, diffuse-in-aggregates and in short narrow tangential bands. Rays of two distinct sizes, uniseriates and very wide and high multiseriates, the latter partly compound. *Quercus calliprinos* has diffuse-porous wood (Plate 4), while *Q. ithaburensis* (Plate 5), *Q. boissieri* and *Q. libani* have ring-, sometimes semi-ring-porous wood.

Moraceae

Ficus carica (Plate 6): Fibres very thick-walled, in wide bands alternating with parenchyma bands. Inter-vessel pits with slit-like, very often coalescent apertures. Rays 1–4 cells wide, up to 45 cells (0.8 mm) high, heterocellular, composed of procumbent central cells and square and upright marginal cells. The specimens are severely shrunken, especially their parenchyma bands.

Myrtaceae

Myrtus (Plate 7): Vessels diffuse, predominantly solitary, occasionally in pairs, of a small diameter; walls with fine, not always distinguishable spiral thickenings; perforation plates simple. Fibres with distinctly bordered pits. Rays 1–2(3) cells wide, up to 20 cells high, heterocellular.

Oleaceae

Fraxinus syriaca (Plate 8; Photo 22): Wood ring-porous. Vessels solitary, in radial multiples of 2–3(4) or rarely in small clusters. Many vessels with tyloses. Parenchyma vasicentric in the earlywood, aliform and confluent towards the end of growth rings, and marginal. Rays 1–4(5) cells wide, up to 20 cells high; homocellular, composed of procumbent cells.

Jasminum: Wood ring-porous. Vessels of latewood solitary and of a small diameter. Part of the vessels and fibres with fine spiral thickenings. Fibres with bordered pits.

Table 9: Distribution of identified taxa of Area C.

Taxonomic identification	V-5		V-5/6		V-6		Total		Jordan River Bank	
	N	%	N	%	N	%	N	%	N	%
Cedrus sp.	1	14.29	1	7.14			2	7.14	1	25.00
Ficus carica	1	14.29					1	3.57		
Fraxinus syriaca	2	28.57	6	42.86	4	57.14	12	42.86	1	25.00
Fraxinus?					1	14.29	1	3.57		
Hedera sp.									1	25.00
Juniperus sp.					1	14.29	1	3.57		
Olea europaea	1	14.29					1	3.57		
Olea?			1	7.14			1	3.57		
Quercus ithaburensis	1	14.29	1	7.14			2	7.14		
Quercus (ithaburensis?)									1	25.00
Salix sp.			1	7.14			1	3.57		
Salix with bark			2	14.29			2	7.14		
Ulmus sp.					1	14.29	1	3.57		
bark	1	14.29	2	14.29			3	10.71		
Total	7	100.0	14	100.0	7	100.0	28	99.98	4	100.0

Table 10: Distribution of identified taxa in layers of Trench I.

Taxonomic identification	I-4		I-4/5		I-5		Trench I	
	N	%	N	%	N	%	N	%
Ficus carica?							1	14.29
Fraxinus syriaca	7	53.85	1	33.33	4	30.77	1	14.29
Fraxinus?	3	23.08	1	33.33	1	7.69		
Juniperus sp.	1	7.69					1	14.29
Myrtus?					1	7.69		
Olea europaea							2	28.57
Populus sp.								
Pyrus sp.					1	7.69		
Quercus calliprinos								
Quercus (ithaburensis?)	1	7.69						
Salix sp.					2	15.38	1	14.29
Salix?	1	7.69	1	33.33	2	15.38		
Vitis sp.								
unknown tree								
bark					2	15.38	1	14.29
Total	13	100.0	3	100.0	13	100.0	7	100.0

Table 11: Distribution of identified taxa in layers of Trenches II and VI.

Taxonomic identification	Trench II		VI-14		Trench VI	
	N	%	N	%	N	%
Ficus carica?						
Fraxinus syriaca	1	25.00	6	43	1	50.00
Fraxinus?			2	14		
Juniperus sp.						
Myrtus?						
Olea europaea			2	14		
Populus sp.			2	14		
Pyrus sp.						
Quercus calliprinos	1	25.00				
Quercus (ithaburensis?)						
Salix sp.						
Salix?						
Vitis sp.	2	50.00				
unknown tree					1	50.00
bark			2	14		
Total	4	100.0	14	100	2	100.0

Table 12: Distribution of identified taxa in layers of Trench II.

Taxonomic identification	II-1		II-2		II-2/3		II-3		II-3/4		II-4		II-4/5	
	N	%	N	%	N	%	N	%	N	%	N	%	N	%
Amygdalus (korschinskii?)														
Cerasus sp.														
Cerasus ?			1	1.85										
Crataegus sp.			1	1.85										
Ficus carica?			1	1.85										
Fraxinus syriaca	2	33.33	27	50.0	8	57.14					2	40.0		
Fraxinus?			3	5.55	1	7.14							1	50
Jasminum sp.			1	1.85										
Jasminum?														
Lonicera sp.														
Lonicera?														
Lycium sp.									1	25.0				
Lycium?														
Myrtus sp.			2	3.7										
Myrtus?											1	20.0		
Nerium?														
Olea europaea	1	16.67	4	7.41					1	25.0				
Olea?							1	50.0						
Periploca?														
Pistacia sp.					1	7.14								
Pistacia?														
Pistacia atlantica			1	1.85	1	7.14								
Pistacia (atlantica?)														
Pistacia atlantica/vera														
Pistacia (palaestina?)														
Pistacia vera														
Pistacia (vera?)														
Populus sp.														
Populus?														
Pyrus sp.			1	1.85					1	25.0				
Pyrus?														
Quercus calliprinos	1	16.67					1	50.0						
Quercus (calliprinos?)														
Quercus ithaburensis									1	25.0				
Quercus ithaburensis/ calliprinos			1	1.85										
Rhus pentaphylla/tripartita														
Rhus?														
Rosaceae, Prunoideae														
Salicaceae?														
Salix sp.	2	33.33	3	5.55	1	7.14								
Salix?														
Ulmus sp.														
Vitis sp.														
Ziziphus/Paliurus														
unknown tree			1	1.85							1	20.0	1	50.0
bark			7	12.96	2	14.29					1	20.0		
bark?														
Total	6	100.0	54	99.97	14	100.0	2	100.0	4	100.0	5	100.0	2	100.0

Table 12 (continued)

Taxonomic identification	II-5		II-5/6		II-6		II-6/7		II-7		II-7/8		II-12		II-14	
	N	%	N	%	N	%	N	%	N	%	N	%	N	%	N	%
Amygdalus (korschinskii?)					1	0.26										
Cerasus sp.			1	4.34												
Cerasus ?																
Crataegus sp.	1	2.56			2	0.53										
Ficus carica?																
Fraxinus syriaca	17	43.59	14	60.87	116	30.93			1	50.00						
Fraxinus?	3	7.69			9	2.40					1	16.67				
Jasminum sp.																
Jasminum?					1	0.26										
Lonicera sp.					5	1.33										
Lonicera?					2	0.53										
Lycium?					3	0.80										
Lycium?																
Myrtus sp.	1	2.56	1	4.34	3	0.80										
Nerium?					1	0.26										
Nerium?																
Olea europaea	4	10.26	1	4.34	25	6.66										
Olea?	4	10.26	1	4.34	8	2.13										
Periploca?					1	0.26										
Pistacia sp.					2	0.53										
Pistacia?	1	2.56	1	4.34	1	0.26										
Pistacia atlantica					16	4.26									2	66.67
Pistacia (atlantica?)					2	0.53										
Pistacia atlantica/vera	1	2.56			4	1.04									1	33.33
Pistacia (palaestina?)					1	0.26										
Pistacia vera					2	0.53										
Pistacia (vera?)					2	0.53										
Populus sp.					2	0.53										
Populus?					1	0.26										
Pyrus sp.	1	2.56			2	0.53	1	100.0								
Pyrus?					2	0.53										
Quercus calliprinos	1	2.56			17	4.53										
Quercus (calliprinos?)					3	0.80										
Quercus ithaburensis					19	5.06							1	100.0		
Quercus ithaburensis/ calliprinos			1	4.34	4	1.06										
Rhus pentaphylla/tripartita					1	0.26										
Rhus?					1	0.26										
Rosaceae, Prunoideae					3	0.80										
Salicaceae?					2	0.53										
Salix sp.	1	2.56	1	4.34	5	1.33			1	50.00	5	83.33				
Salix?	1	2.56			1	0.26										
Ulmus sp.					13	3.46										
Vitis sp.																
Ziziphus/Paliurus					2	0.53										
unknown tree			1	4.34	8	2.13										
bark	3	7.69	1	4.34	75	20.00										
bark?					7	1.86										
Total	39	99.97	23	99.93	373	99.98	1	100.0	2	100.0	6	100.0	1	100.0	3	100.0

Table 13: Distribution of identified taxa in Layer II-6 (per level).

Taxonomic identification	II-6 level 1		II-6 level 2		II-6 level 3		II-6 level 4		II-6 level 5		II-6 level 6		II-6 level 7	
	N	%	N	%	N	%	N	%	N	%	N	%	N	%
Amygdalus (korschinskii?)													1	1.25
Crataegus sp.	2	1.39												
Fraxinus syriaca	54	37.76	20	29.41	5	23.81	3	7.32	1	25.00			28	35.00
Fraxinus syriaca with bark					1	4.76								
Fraxinus?	7	4.89	2	2.94										
Jasminum?									1	25.00				
Lonicera sp.			1	1.47									4	5.00
Lonicera?	2	1.39												
Lycium?			3	4.41										
Myrtus sp.	1	0.69					1	2.44					1	1.25
Nerium?	1	0.69												
Olea europaea	14	9.79	6	8.82	1	4.76							3	3.75
Olea europaea with bark	1	0.69												
Olea?	4	2.79	1	1.47	1	4.76	1	2.44					1	1.25
Periploca?	1	0.69												
Pistacia sp.							2	4.88						
Pistacia?	1	0.69												
Pistacia atlantica	9	6.29	2	2.94	1	4.76	3	7.32					1	1.25
Pistacia (atlantica?)	2	1.39												
Pistacia atlantica/vera	1	0.69	1	1.47			2	4.88			1	33.33		
Pistacia (palaestina?)							1	2.44						
Pistacia (vera?)	1	0.69					1	2.44						
Populus sp.			1	1.47			1	2.44						
Populus?			1	1.47										
Pyrus sp.	2	1.39												
Pyrus?	2	1.39												
Quercus sp.	1	0.69												
Quercus calliprinos	5	3.49	5	7.35	1	4.76	3	7.32					2	2.50
Quercus (calliprinos?)	1	0.69					2	4.88						
Quercus ithaburensis	6	4.19	1	1.47			6	14.63	1	25.00			4	5.00
Quercus ithaburensis/ calliprinos							3	7.32						
Rhus pentaphylla/tripartita			1	1.47										
Rhus?					1	4.76								
Rosaceae, Prunoideae	3	2.09												
Salicaceae?	2	1.39												
Salix sp.	2	1.39	2	2.94										
Salix with bark									1	25.00				
Salix?			1	1.47										
Ulmus sp.			1	1.47			1	2.44			1	33.33	10	12.50
Ziziphus/Paliurus	1	0.69	1	1.47										
unknown tree	5	3.49	3	4.41										
bark	11	7.69	14	20.59	10	47.62	11	26.83			1	33.33	20	25.00
bark?	1	0.69	1	1.47									5	6.25
Total	142	99.79	68	100.0	21	100.0	41	100.0	4	100.0	3	100.0	80	100.0

Table 14: Distribution of the identified taxa in the different layers and levels.

Taxonomic identification	N	Location
Amygdalus (*korschinskii*?)	1	II-6 level 7
Cedrus sp.	2	V-5; V-5/6
Cerasus sp.	1	II-5/6
Cerasus?	1	II-2
Crataegus sp.	4	II-2; II-5; II-6 level 1
Ficus carica	2	II-2; V-5
Ficus carica?	1	Trench I
Fraxinus syriaca	245	II-1; II-2; II-2/3; II-4; II-5; II-5/6; II-6 levels 1-5. 7; II-6/7; II-7; I-4; I-4/5; I-5; Trenches I; VI; VI-14; II; V-5; V-5/6; V-6
Fraxinus?	28	II-2; II-2/3
Hedera sp.	1	V-5/V-6
Jasminum sp.	1	II-2
Jasminum?	1	II-6 level 5
Juniperus sp.	3	I-4; Trench I; V-6
Lonicera sp.	5	II-6 levels 2, 7
Lonicera?	2	II-6 level 1
Lycium sp.	1	II-3/4
Lycium?	3	II-6 level 2
Myrtus sp.	7	II-2; II-5; II-6 levels 1, 4, 7; II-6/7
Myrtus?	2	II-4; I-5
Nerium?	1	II-7
Olea europaea	45	II-1; II-2; II-3/4; II-5; II-6 levels 1-3, 7; II-6/7; Trench I; VI-14; V-5
Olea?	15	II-3; II-5; II-5/6; II-6 level 1, 7; V-5/6
Periploca?	1	II-6 level 1
Pistacia sp.	4	II-2/3; II-6 level 4; II-6/7
Pistacia?	3	II-5; II-6 level 1
Pistacia atlantica	25	II-2; II-3; II-6 levels 1-4, 7; II-7; II-14
Pistacia (*atlantica*?)	2	II-6 level 1
Pistacia atlantica/vera	8	II-5; II-6 levels 2, 4, 6; 7; II-7; II-14
Pistacia (*palaestina*?)	1	II-6 level 4
Pistacia vera	3	II-6 level 7
Pistacia (*vera*?)	2	II-6 levels 1, 4
Populus sp.	4	II-6 levels 2, 4; VI-14
Populus?	1	II-6 level 2
Pyrus sp.	6	II-2; II-3/4
Pyrus?	2	II-6 level 1
Quercus calliprinos	27	II-1; II-3; II-5; II-6 levels 1-4, 7; II-7; Trench II
Quercus (*calliprinos*?)	3	II-6 levels 1, 4
Quercus ithaburensis	26	II-3/4; II-6 levels 1, 2, 4, 5, 7; II-12
Quercus (*ithaburensis*?)	2	I-4
Quercus sp.	11	II-2; II-5/6; II-6 level 4, 7;
Rhus pentaphylla/tripartita	2	II-2; II-6 level 2
Rhus pentaphylla/tripartita?	1	no data
Rhus?	1	II-6 level 3
Rosaceae, Prunoideae	1	II-6 level 3
Salicaceae?	1	II-6 level 1
Salix sp.	26	II-1; II-2; II-2/3; II-5; II-6 levels 1-2, 5, 7; II-6/7; II-7/8; I-5; Trench I; V-5/6
Salix?	8	II-5; II-6 level 2; I-4; I-4/5; I-6
Salix/Populus	4	II-6 level 1
Ulmus sp.	14	II-6 levels 2, 4, 6, 7; V-6
Vitis sp.	2	Trench II
Ziziphus/Paliurus	2	II-6 levels 1, 2
unknown tree	13	II-2; II-4; II-4/5; II-5/6; II-6 levels 1-2, 7; II-7; Trench VI
bark	97	II-2; II-2/3; II-4; II-5; II-5/6; II-6 levels 1-4, 6,7; II-7; I-5; Trench I; VI-14; V-5; V-5/6
bark?	7	II-6 levels 1, 2, 7

40

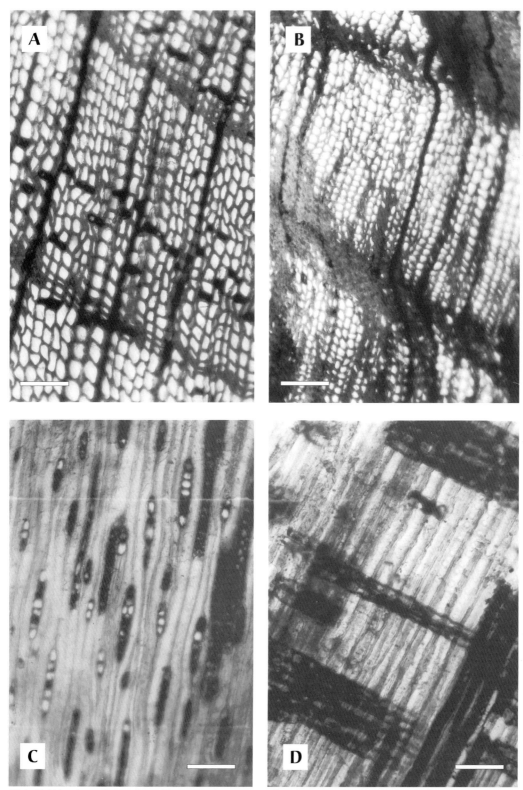

Plate 3: Wood specimens identified as *Juniperus*. A and B. Cross sections. C. Tangential section.
D. Radial section. Scale bars of A, B, C, D=100 µm.

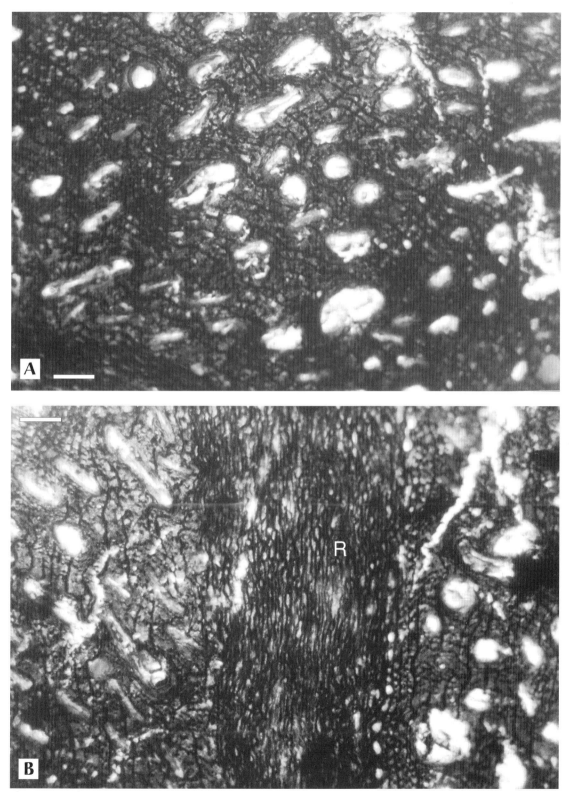

Plate 4: Wood specimen identified as *Quercus calliprinos*. A and B. Cross sections. A showing diffuse-porous wood. In B a multicellular ray (R) can be observed. Scale bars of A, B=200 μm.

42

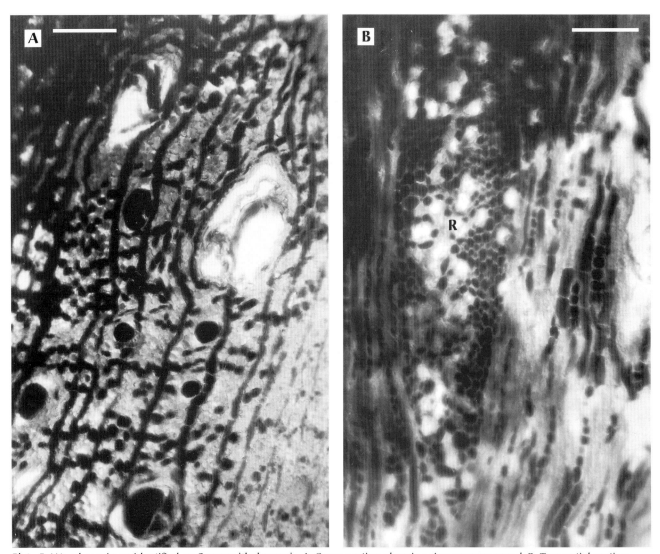

Plate 5: Wood specimen identified as *Quercus ithaburensis*. A. Cross section showing ring-porous wood. B. Tangential section showing uniseriate rays and one multiseriate ray (R). Scale bars of A, B=100 μm.

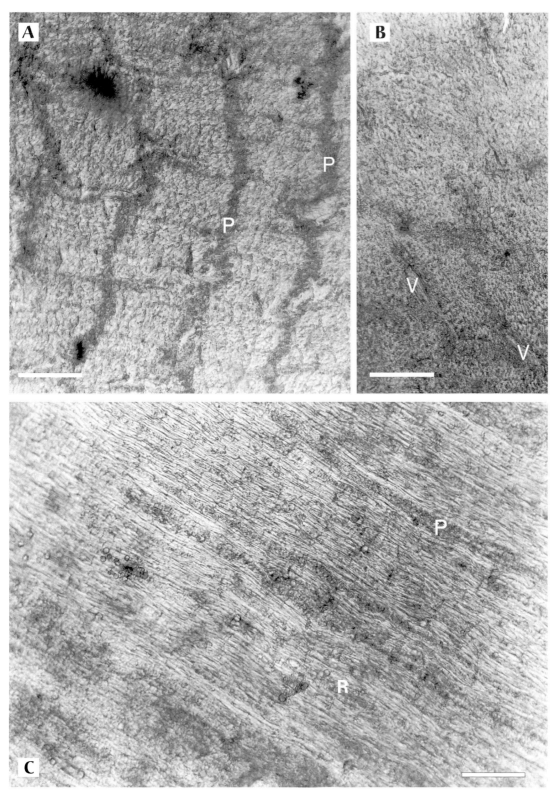

Plate 6: Wood specimen identified as *Ficus carica*, with wood strongly compressed. A and B. Cross sections. C. Tangential section. P - parenchyma strands; R - ray; V - vessels. Scale bars of A, B, C=100 μm.

44

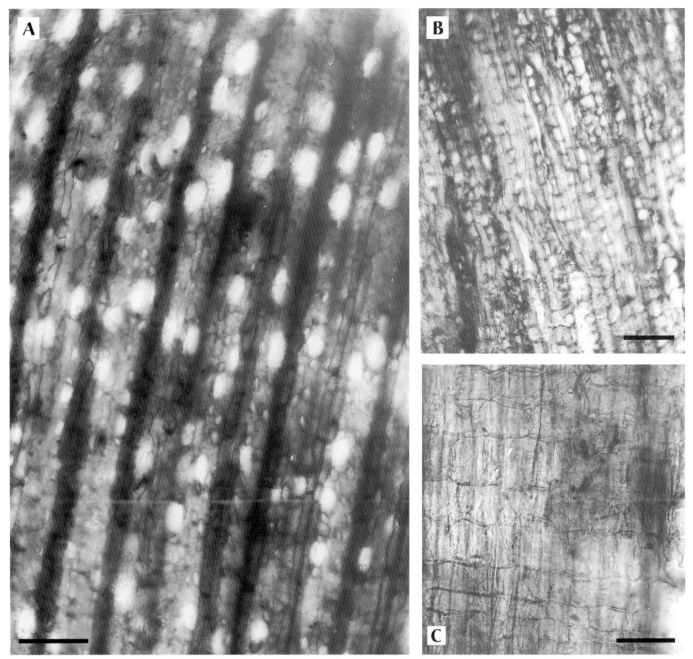

Plate 7: Wood specimens identified as *Myrtus*. A. Cross section. B. Tangential section. C. Radial section. Scale bars of A, B=100 μm; C=50 μm.

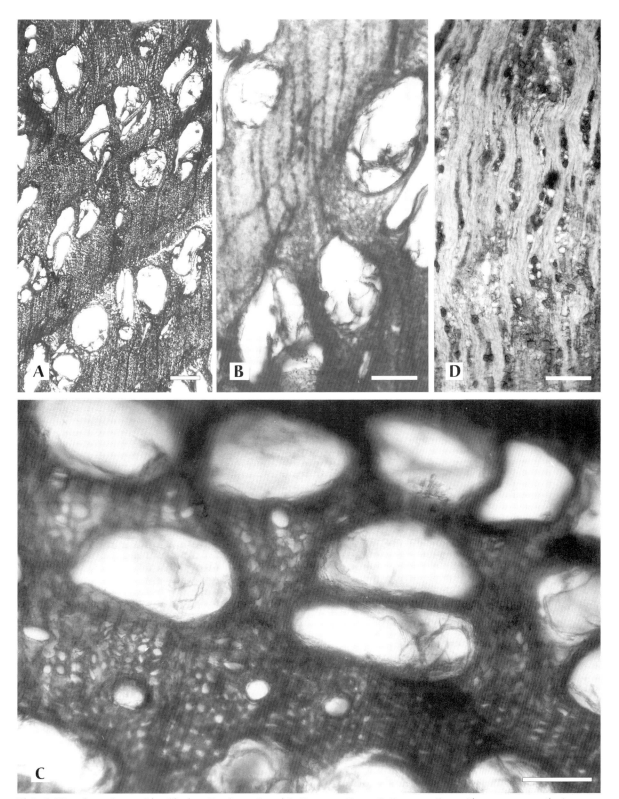

Plate 8: Wood specimens identified as *Fraxinus*. A and B. Cross sections. C. Cross section with narrow growth rings. D. Tangential section, with shrunken wood. Scale bars of A=200 µm; B, C, D=100 µm.

Photo 22: Section of wood (*Fraxinus syriaca*) excavated from Layer II-6 level 1.

Rays mainly uniseriate, heterocellular with upright and square marginal cells and weakly procumbent central cells. *Olea europaea* (Plate 9): Growth rings distinct to faint. Vessels diffuse, solitary, in radial multiples of 2–4(6) occasionally in clusters; angular to rounded in cross section; diameter up to 70 μm. Some vessels with gummy substances. Rays 1–2 (3)-seriate, heterocellular; some cells crystalliferous. Among those identified as olive wood, some had typical rays up to 12(20) cells high, and others much higher rays and a larger number of uniseriate ones (cf. Werker, 1998).

Pinaceae

Cedrus (Plate 10): A gymnosperm, vascular elements consisting only of tracheids, with mostly uniseriate bordered pits. Axial parenchyma confined to the growth ring boundary. Rays mostly uniseriate, rarely biseriate, (1)3–20(35) cells high composed of marginal ray tracheids in single rows and fairly thick-walled ray parenchyma cells with nodular end walls. Ray tracheids with smooth walls. Each cross-field with 2–4 taxodioid pits (in earlywood). Vertical resin ducts close to each other are of traumatic type, with mostly thick-walled lignified epithelial cells. Vertical resin ducts are more common than horizontal ones within rays.

The two specimens identified as *Cedrus* possess resin ducts and wound tissue in many of their growth rings.

Rhamnaceae

Paliurus: see *Ziziphus*

Ziziphus/Paliurus: Vessels diffuse; solitary, in radial multiples of 2–3, occasionally in small clusters. Fibres medium-thick to very thick-walled. Rays 1(2) up to 20(24) cells high; weakly heterocellular composed of square, upright and infrequent weakly procumbent cells.

Rosaceae

Amygdalus korschinskii: Wood ring-porous. Vessels mostly solitary, widely spaced in latewood; with fine spiral thickenings. Fibres with distinctly bordered pits in radial and tangential walls. Rays 1(2)-seriate and 3–8-seriate, the latter up to 44 cells high, rarely compound; heterocellular, composed mainly of procumbent cells and weakly procumbent to upright marginal cells.

Cerasus: Growth rings distinct. Wood ring-porous. Vessels mostly solitary, occasionally in variously directed multiples of 2–3; with prominent spiral thickenings. Inter-vessel pits round, diffuse. Fibres very thick-walled, with distinctly bordered pits in radial and tangential walls, occasionally with spiral thickenings. Rays 1–3-seriate up to 0.8 mm or more in height; heterocellular, composed of square, weakly procumbent and upright cells.

Crataegus (Plate 11): Growth rings distinct. Vessels diffuse, densely arranged, mostly solitary, and mostly angular in cross section. Fibres thick-walled with distinctly bordered pits in the radial and tangential walls. Apotracheal parenchyma diffuse, sometimes diffuse-in-aggregates. Rays 1–3(4) cells wide up to 25(35) cells high;

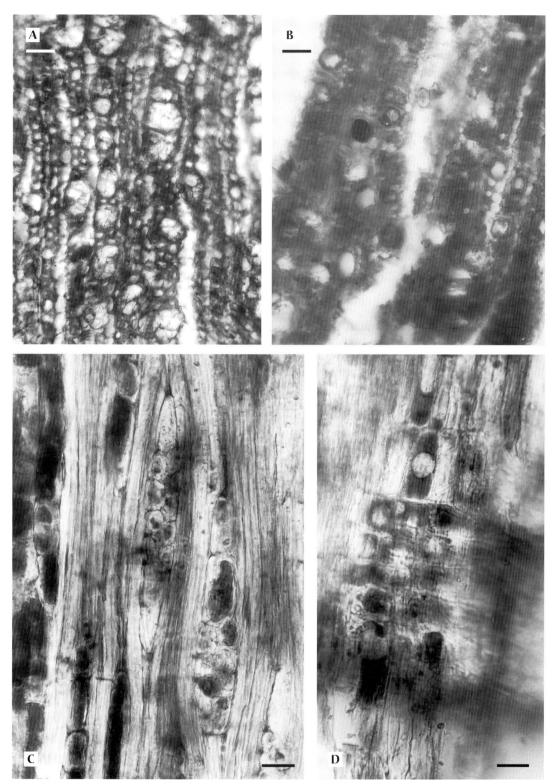

Plate 9: Wood specimens identified as *Olea*. A and B. Cross sections of two specimens. C. Tangential section showing heterogeneous rays. D. Radial section showing a heterogeneous ray. Scale bars of A, B=50 μm; C, D=25 μm.

48

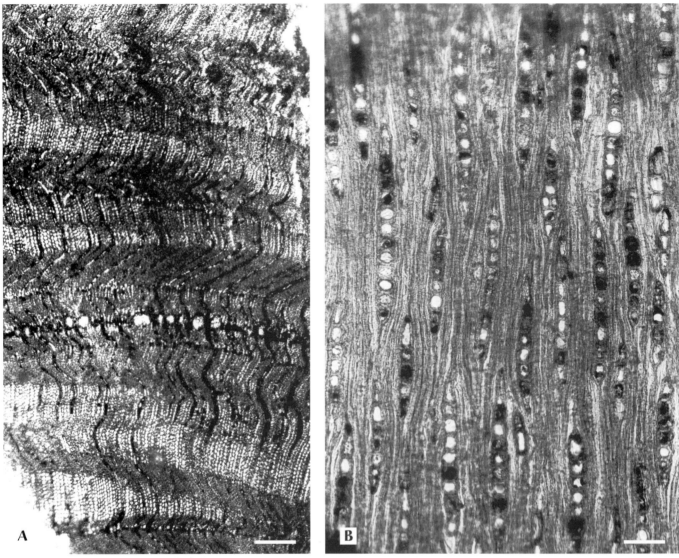

Plate 10: Wood specimens identified as *Cedrus*. A. Cross section with a tangential row of resin ducts in one of the growth rings. B. Tangential section. Scale bars of A=200 μm; B=50 μm.

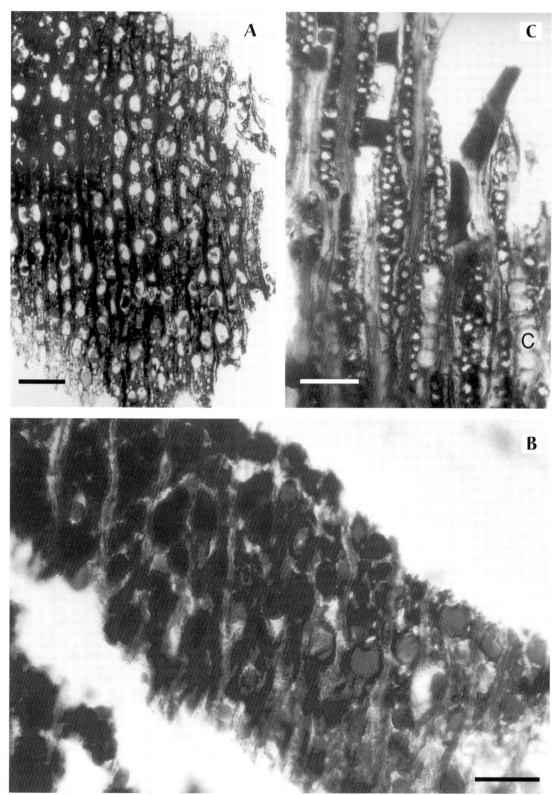

Plate 11: Wood specimen identified as *Crataegus*. A and B. Cross sections. C. Tangential section showing a row of large cells which contained crystals (C). Scale bars of A=200 μm; B, C=100 μm.

predominantly homocellular consisting of procumbent cells. Crystals solitary, prismatic in enlarged chambered parenchyma cells.

Pyrus syriaca (Plate 12): Growth rings distinct. Vessels diffuse, almost exclusively solitary, rarely in pairs or small clusters, angular in cross section; many vessels with gummy contents. Fibres with distinctly bordered pits. Apotracheal parenchyma diffuse to diffuse-in-aggregates. Rays 1–2(3)-seriate up to 43(55) cells high; predominantly homocellular, composed of procumbent cells, occasionally with square or weakly upright marginal cells. Crystals very infrequent in chambered, not enlarged parenchyma cells. Rosaceae, Prunoideae (Plate 13): Semi-ring-porous. Vessels with fine spiral thickenings. Vasicentric tracheids present. Rays wide and quite high. Fibres with bordered pits.

Salicaceae

Populus euphratica/*Salix* spp.: Growth rings distinct. Vessels diffuse, solitary, in radial multiples of 2–3(4), occasionally in small clusters. Fibres thin- to medium-thick-walled. Rays uniseriate, very rarely biseriate; ray-vessel pits in cross-fields sometimes giving a reticulate appearance (Plate 14).

The difference between *Populus* and *Salix* is that in *Populus* the rays are typically homocellular, sometimes with marginal cells somewhat less procumbent than the central cells or square, while in *Salix* many rays are heterocellular, composed of 1–3 rows of upright, sometimes irregularly shaped marginal cells and procumbent or sometimes square and even upright central cells (Plate 14C). Finding an anatomical feature in a section which is absent in one species and frequent in another is a positive proof for identification of the latter (*Salix*), but not finding it is not always a reliable criterion for identification of the former (*Populus*). Therefore, distinction between the two genera is sometimes uncertain.

Solanaceae

Lycium (Plate 15): Vessels form a dendritic pattern, wider vessels are clustered with very narrow ones intergrading with vascular tracheids. Rays mostly uniseriate.

Ulmaceae

Ulmus (Plate 16): Wood ring-porous. Earlywood vessels large, solitary or in pairs, with vasicentric parenchyma; latewood vessels small, in many-celled clusters forming tangential to oblique bands together with vascular tracheids and paratracheal parenchyma. Walls of smaller vessels and fibre tracheids with fine spiral thickenings. Tyloses may be present. Parenchyma vasicentric around large vessels and around the bands of the small ones. Rays 1–6-seriate, up to 100 cells high, homocellular, with strongly procumbent cells, sometimes weakly heterocellular with weakly procumbent or square marginal cells. Solitary prismatic crystals are present in longitudinal chains of parenchymatic cells. According to Schweingruber (1990), it is difficult to distinguish between species.

Vitaceae

Vitis (Plate 17): Wood ring- to semi-ring-porous. Vessels mostly in radial multiples of 2–15 and in clusters together with vascular tracheids. Perforations simple but scalariform in some of the narrow vessels. Inter-vessel pits scalariform, in larger vessels in several rows. Vascular tracheids and occasionally narrow vessels with irregular, very fine spiral thickenings. Fibres septate. Rays (3)7–13 cells wide and very high, heterocellular, with mostly procumbent cells and some square or upright cells.

Affinities Unknown

'Unknown tree' (Plates 18–20): The vessels form a dendritic, sometimes radial or tangential pattern, together with paratracheal parenchyma and vascular tracheids; vessels are mainly rounded in cross section, with maximal radial diameter of ca. 100 μm. Walls of some vascular tracheids and vessels with spiral thickenings. Apotracheal parenchyma in more or less tangential bands, up to 5 cells wide, and marginal parenchyma 1–2(4) cells wide. Fibres thick- to very thick-walled alternating with parenchyma bands. Rays 1–3(4)-seriate up to ca. 20 cells high; heterocellular, composed of procumbent and square central cells and square to upright marginal cells. Many vessels as well as parenchyma and ray cells with dark materials.

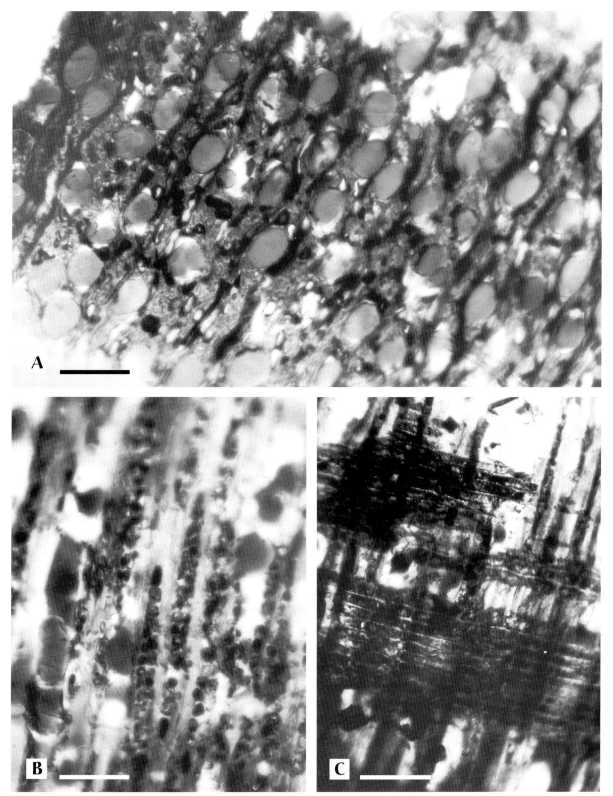

Plate 12: Wood specimen identified as *Pyrus*. A. Cross section. B. Tangential section. C. Radial section. Scale bars of A, B, C=100 μm.

52

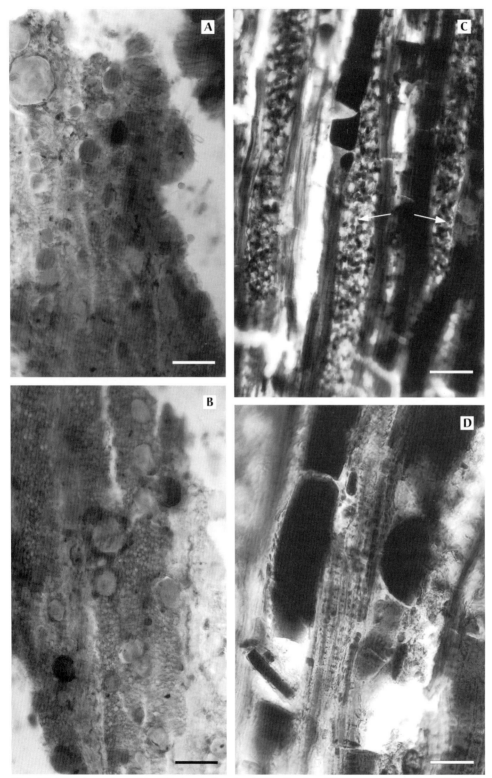

Plate 13: Wood specimen identified as belonging to the family of Rosaceae, Prunoideae. A. and B. Cross sections. C. Tangential section showing very high rays (arrows). D. Vasicentric tracheids close to vessels which are filled with dark materials. Scale bars of A, B, C=100 μm; D=50 μm.

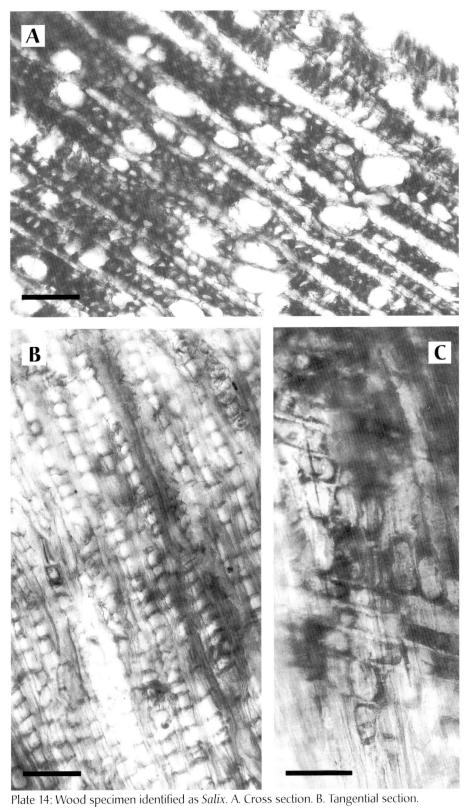

Plate 14: Wood specimen identified as *Salix*. A. Cross section. B. Tangential section.
C. Radial section. Scale bars of A, B, C=100 μm.

54

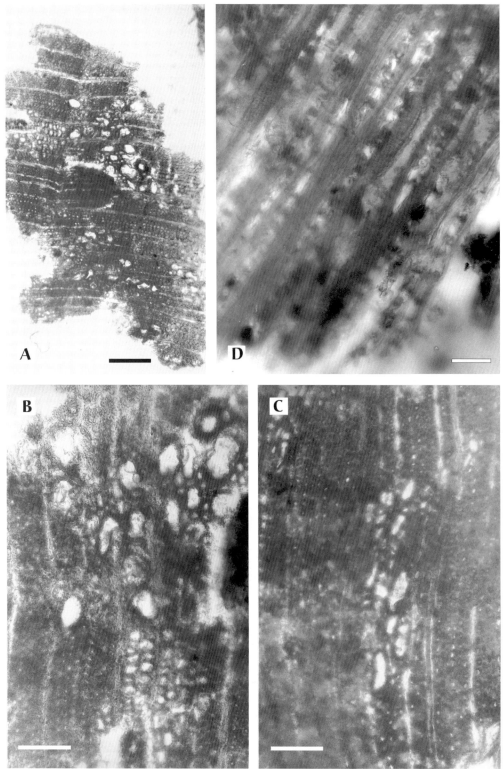

Plate 15: Wood specimen identified as *Lycium*. A-C. Cross section. B and C enlargements of A. D. Tangential section. Scale bars of A=200 μm; B, C=100μm; D=25 μm.

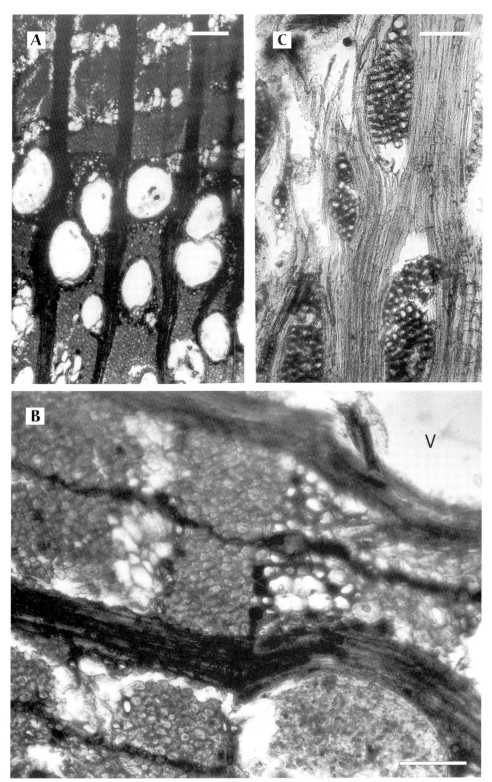

Plate 16: Wood specimen identified as *Ulmus*. A and B. Cross sections. A. Showing the border between two growth rings. B. Showing tangential strands of small vessels; V - large vessel of early wood. C. Tangential section. Scale bars of A=200 μm; B, C=100 μm.

56

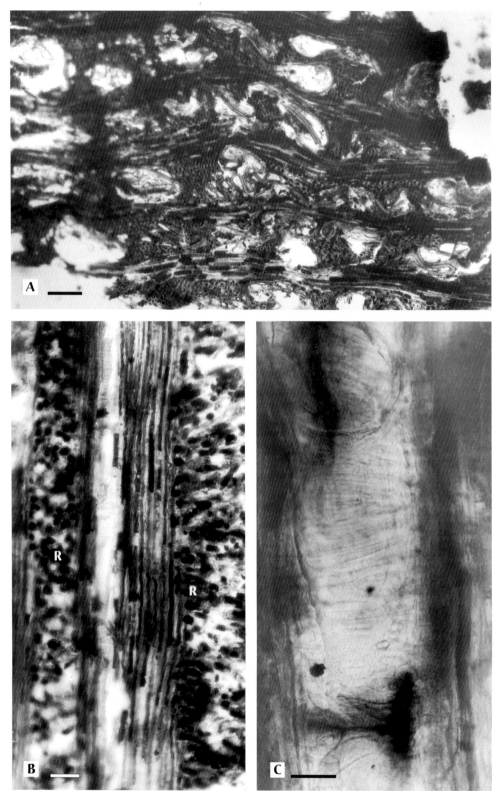

Plate 17: Wood specimen identified as *Vitis*. A. Cross section. B. Tangential section showing part of high rays (R). C. Vessel member with scalariform pits. Scale bars of A, B, C=50 μm.

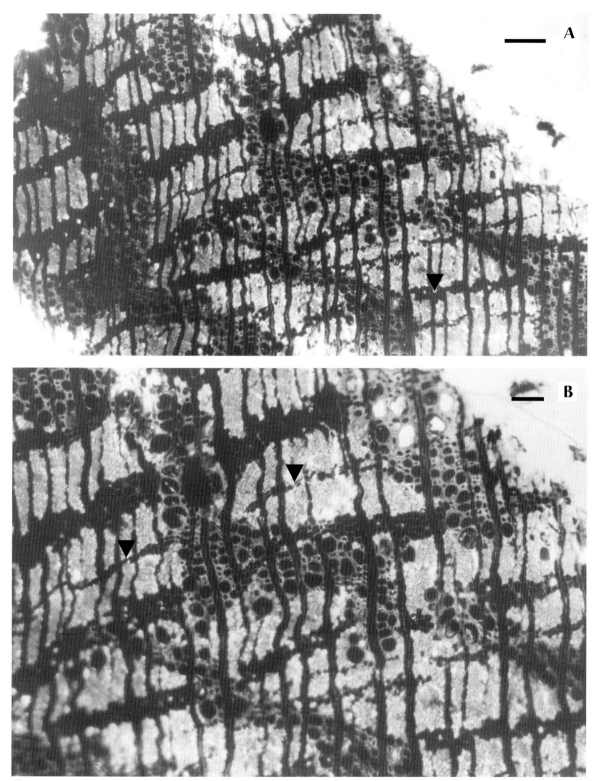

Plate 18: Wood of unidentified tree ('unknown'). A. Cross sections showing tangential parenchyma bands; the narrow ones (arrowheads) apparently marginal parenchyma between growth rings. B. Enlargement of A. Scale bars of A=200 μm; B=100 μm.

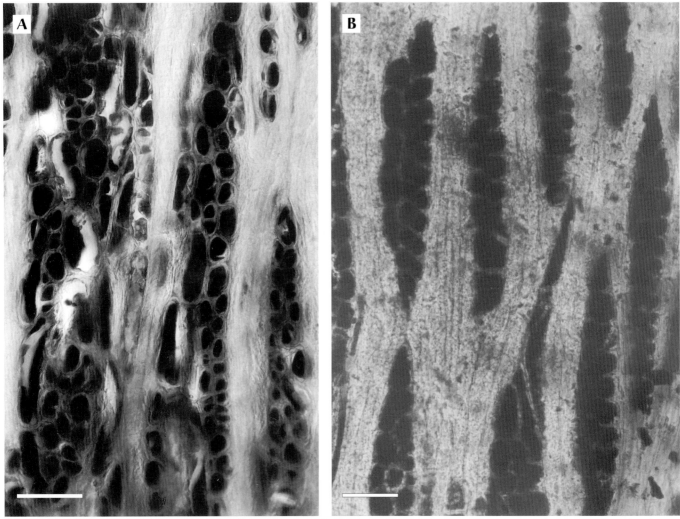

Plate 19: Wood of unidentified tree ('unknown'); tangential sections. A. Showing rays partly at a parenchyma strand. B. Showing rays at a fibre strand. Scale bars of A, B=50 µm.

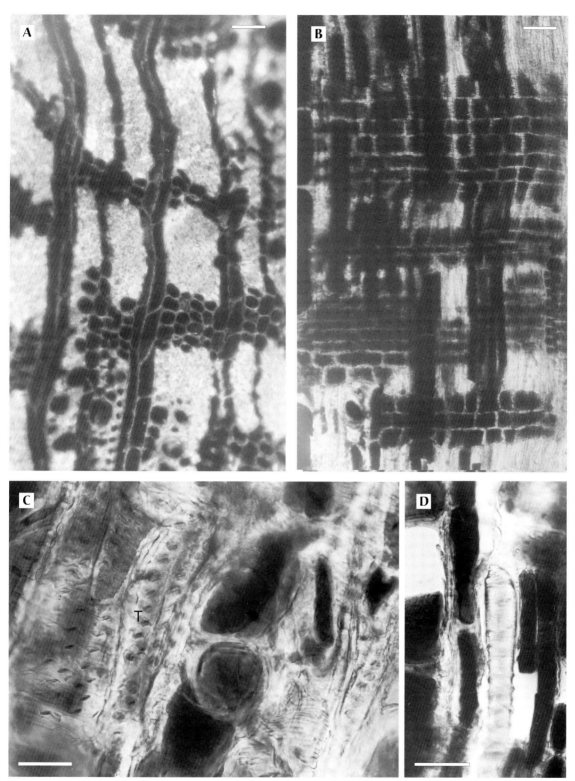

Plate 20: Wood of unidentified tree ('unknown'). A. Cross section. B. Radial section. C. Longitudinal section
showing vasicentric tracheids with bordered pits (T) and vessels with secondary spiral thickening.
D. Tracheary element with secondary spiral thickening. Scale bars of A, B=50 μm; C, D=25 μm.

Of the trees growing in the region, this type of wood most resembles that of *Retama raetam* (Legumniosae) but differs from it in the following features: its vessels and parenchyma cells are not storied; the apotracheal parenchyma bands are 1–5 cells wide while those of *Retama* are 1–2(4). The wood of the 'unknown tree' also resembles *Phillyrea* in its dendritic vessel arrangement and initial parenchyma but differs from it in vessel diameter and the absence in *Phillyrea* of parenchyma bands.

Limitations of Identification According to Wood Anatomy

Taxonomic identification by wood anatomy is of great value, but has its limitations. Wood anatomy can lead to the identification of different levels of taxa according to a similarity of anatomical characteristics, within a family, a group of genera or between the species of a genus. On the other hand, sometimes 'woods belonging to different botanical families may superficially appear similar because there has been considerable convergent and parallel evolution in wood structure' (Wheeler and Bass, 1998: 247). In ancient material that is not always consistently preserved, fine anatomical characteristics which can help in distinguishing between such families may be obscured. Moreover, intraspecific variations may also cause uncertainties in identification. Some of the limitations faced in the botanical identification of the wood material of GBY according to its anatomical characteristics are summarized here.

a) Of the four *Quercus* species which grow nowadays in the region, *Q. calliprinos* has diffuse-porous wood while *Q. boissieri*, *Q. ithaburensis* and *Q. libani* have ring-porous and sometimes semi-ring-porous wood. Among the ring-porous species, in the first species latewood vessels are often numerous while in the latter two they are infrequent. However, this feature appears to be not always significant. Branches of present-day *Q. ithaburensis* have sometimes been observed to possess numerous vessels (Lev-Yadun, per. comm.). Other species with similar characteristics also grow in Europe. It cannot therefore absolutely be ruled out that other species of oak grew half a million years ago in

the region. The definitions of *Q. calliprinos*-type and *Q. ithaburensis*-type are therefore preferable. For certain specimens the distinction between diffuse- and ring-porous wood is not clear enough for definition of the species type.

b) Among the examined material, two types of anatomical characteristics were identified as *Olea europaea*; one has short rays, many of which are biseriate, and one has long rays with a larger proportion of uniseriate rays. Due to the antiquity of the material, this cannot be a feature differentiating the wild type from the contemporary cultivated type, one of the possible causes suggested for such a difference (Werker, 1998).

c) It is very difficult to distinguish between species of the genera *Lycium* and *Salix*.

d) No distinction can be made between species of *Crataegus*.

e) The two species of *Ziziphus* which grow in the region, *Z. spina-christi* and *Z. lotus*, and *Paliurus spina-christi*, all of the Rhamnaceae, are very similar in their wood anatomy and therefore cannot be separated (Fahn et al., 1986; Schweingruber, 1990). It has been suggested by Baruch and Goring-Morris (1997) that distinction between the two genera can be made on the basis of the vessels' form in cross section: angular in *Paliurus* and rounded in *Ziziphus*. However, our reexamination of sections of extant wood could not confirm this.

The segments of the identified plants were from trunks and branches of varying thickness. Due to the relatively short length of the segments, it was difficult to determine morphologically whether some of them may have been roots. The wood anatomy of roots may be similar to that of the above-ground woody parts or different in certain characteristics, depending on the species: intraspecific variations can also be found between different roots of the same plant. The wood of some of the specimens may therefore be that of a root, a fact that can perhaps explain certain variations found in the anatomical structure: 1. In some sections many distortions in wood structure, like circular and stream patterns, were observed (Plate 21A). Such patterns may appear in branch junctions, around and

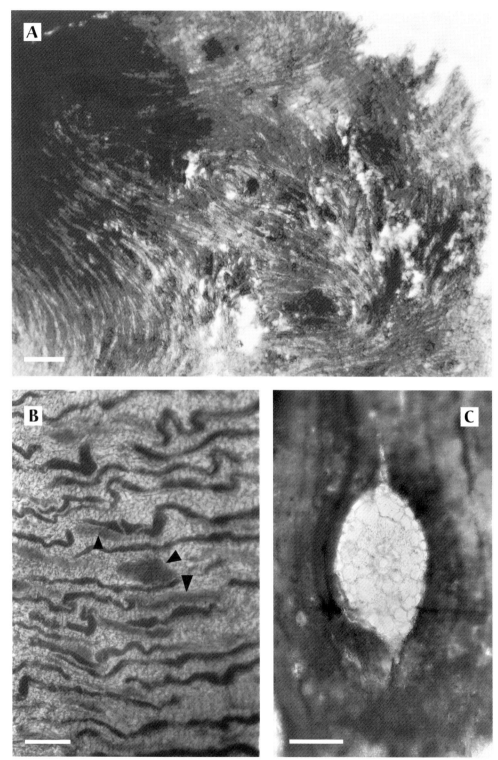

Plate 21: A. Section of wood (from a specimen identified as *Fraxinus*) of a very irregular structure.
B. Cross section of a shrunken wood identified as *Salix* (arrowheads pointing to vessels).
C. Cross section of a specimen identified as *Lycium* penetrated by a contemporary root. Scale
bars of A=200 μm; B=25 μm; C=100 μm. Fig. B from Belitzky et al., 1991.

above developing buds or roots and in wound tissues (Lev-Yadun, 1990 and literature therein). 2. The wood anatomy characteristics usually used for distinction between *Quercus boissieri* on the one hand and *Q. ithaburensis* and *Q. libani* on the other is the numerous and angular to slightly rounded vessels of the first and the infrequent vessels, mostly rounded, of the latter two. Some of the specimens identified as ring-porous oak have a much higher number of vessels than the usual for both *Q. ithaburensis* and *Q. libani*, but they are mostly rounded in cross section. This discrepancy might perhaps indicate the presence of roots among the specimens. The question whether this discrepancy indicates a higher intraspecific variability of wood anatomy in branches or whether these are roots cannot be answered without a thorough examination of comparative wood anatomy of branches and roots of the above three species.

The material included in this analysis is restricted to the wood segments. The bark specimens still await identification.

Present-Day Habitats of the Identified Plants

The plant habitats and phytogeographic zones given below are mainly according to Zohary (1966; 1972) and Feinbrun-Dothan (1978) unless otherwise stated. Only the regions closest to the excavation site are recorded here.

Amygdalus korschinskii is a West Irano-Turanian element; it grows as a tree or high shrub in impoverished maquis and maquis-steppes in Upper Galilee and the upper Jordan Valley (Figure 10). It appears in association with *Pistacia atlantica* on slopes facing the Hula Valley (Rabinovitch-Vin, 1986). It has been suggested (Rabinovitch-Vin, 1977) that a similar kind of steppe-forest may have covered these slopes in the past.

Cedrus libani is an East Mediterranean element. It grows as a tree in a few relict stands (Mikesell, 1969) on mountains of Lebanon and farther away in Cyprus and Turkey.

Cerasus prostrata is a Mediterranean element; it grows as a shrub on rocky ground on Mt. Hermon (Figure 10).

The three *Crataegus* species that grow in Israel are very similar in their wood anatomy and cannot be unambiguously separated. *C. aronia* is an East Mediterranean and West Irano-Turanian element. It grows as a tree or shrub in maquis and maquis-steppes in Upper and Lower Galilee. It accompanies the *Quercus ithaburensis - Pistacia atlantica* association. *Crataegus monogyna* is a Mediterranean and Euro-Siberian element. It grows as a shrub or small tree in oak maquis in shady valleys at about 1000 m asl in Upper Galilee, and is very rare today. *C. azarolus* is an East Mediterranean element growing as a tree in more humid maquis in Upper Galilee.

Ficus carica is a Mediterranean and Irano-Turanian element; it grows as a tree. The uncultivated variety *F. c. caprificus* is native to Upper Galilee (Zohary, 1966).

Fraxinus syriaca is an East Mediterranean and West Irano-Turanian element. It grows as a tree along rivers and streams in the Hula Valley, Upper Galilee, the Beit Shean Valley and the Golan (Figure 11).

Hedera is a Euro-Siberian and Mediterranean element, growing as a climbing shrub on rocks and in maquis in Upper Galilee.

Jasminum fruticans is a Mediterranean and West Irano-Turanian element, growing as a shrub in *Quercetum calliprine* maquis, at an elevation of about 400–1000 m asl in Upper Galilee and the Golan.

Juniperus drupacea is a shrub and *J. excelsa* a tree; both grow on Mt. Hermon (Figure 10). *J. oxycedrus* is a Mediterranean shrub or tree which grows on calcareous soil in Upper Galilee too, but is rare today. The wood anatomy of these *Juniperus* species is very similar and distinction between them based on wood anatomy is unreliable.

Lonicera (Figure 12). The anatomical characteristics of the sample are more similar to European species (wood ring-porous) than the species growing nowadays in the region, *Lonicera etrusca* (wood diffuse-porous). This cannot result from the difference between early- and later-produced growth rings. The five segments were found in two different levels of Layer II-6 (Table 14) and they all belong to a thick branch with many growth rings. *L. etrusca* is a Mediterranean element growing as a climbing shrub in

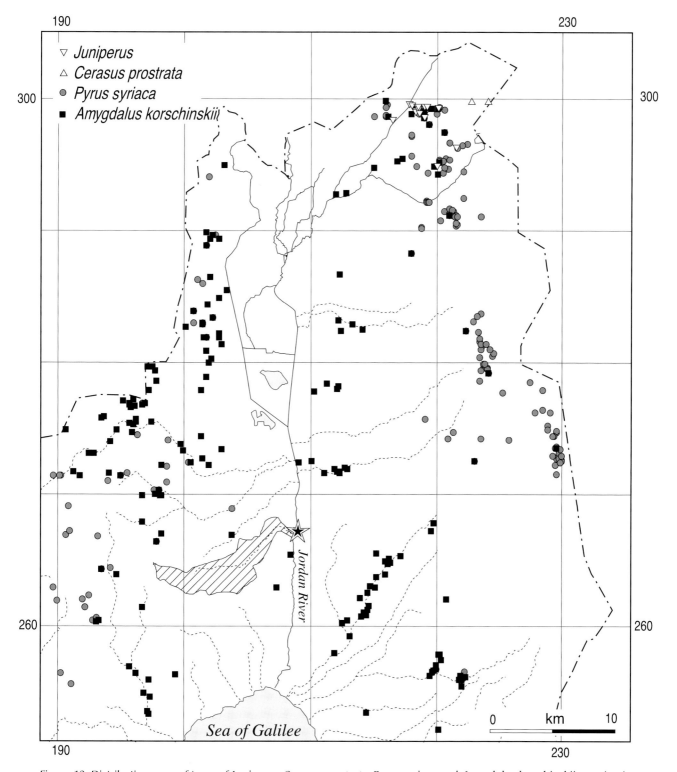

Figure 10: Distribution map of trees of *Juniperus*, *Cerasus prostrata*, *Pyrus syriaca* and *Amygdalus korschinskii* growing in Galilee and the upper Jordan Valley today.

64

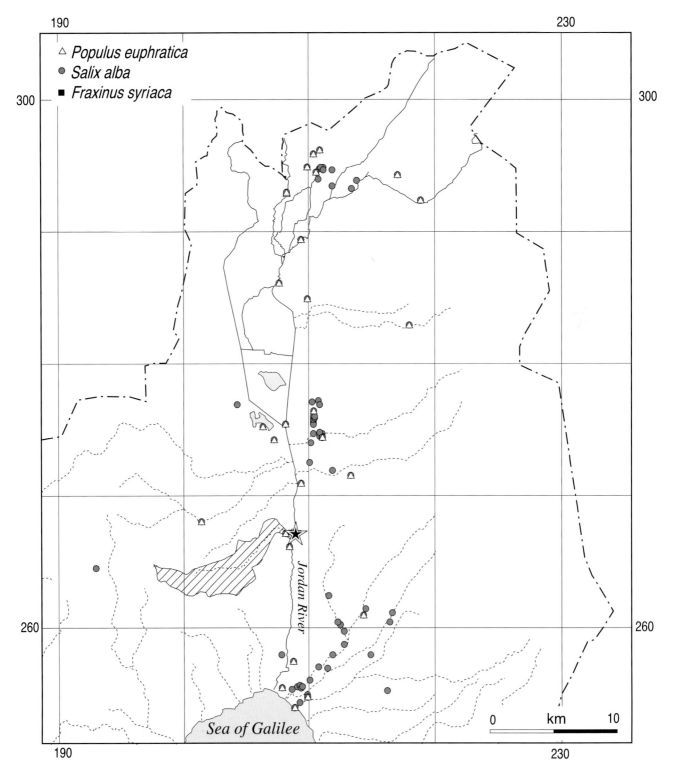

Figure 11: Distribution map of trees of *Populus euphratica, Salix alba* and *Fraxinus syriaca* growing in Galilee and the upper Jordan Valley today.

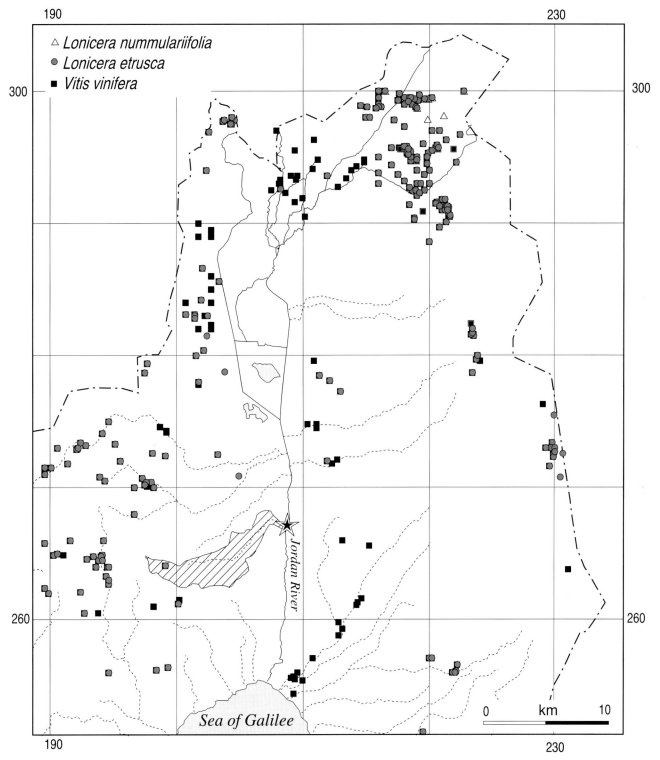

Figure 12: Distribution map of shrubs of *Lonicera nummulariifolia* growing on Mt. Hermon and climbing shrubs of *Lonicera etrusca* and *Vitis vinifera* growing in Galilee and the upper Jordan Valley today.

rocky places in maquis and garigue in Upper and Lower Galilee and the Golan. *L. nummulariifolia* is a shrub that grows on Mt. Hermon; and its wood anatomy could not be examined.

Lycium. It is difficult to separate the four species that grow in Israel according to their wood anatomy. *L. europaeum* is a Mediterranean element, a shrub growing along fields and wadis in Upper and Lower Galilee, the upper Jordan Valley and the Golan. The other species grow in more arid areas further south.

Myrtus communis is a Mediterranean element, a shrub or sometimes a small tree growing in maquis and riverine thickets in Upper Galilee, the Dan Valley and the upper Jordan Valley.

Nerium oleander is a Mediterranean element, a shrub growing on banks of lakes and streams and on stony wadi beds in the upper and lower Hula Plain, the Jordan Valley and the Golan.

Olea europaea is an East Mediterranean element, growing as a tree or shrub. Var. *sylvestris*, the wild olive, grows in maquis in Upper Galilee and the Golan, mainly in the *Quercus calliprinos - Pistacia palaestina* association (Figure 13).

Paliurus: see *Ziziphus*.

Periploca aphylla is a Sudanian element extending into the East Saharo-Arabian region. It grows as a shrub in rocky deserts in the upper and lower Jordan Valley and the Dead Sea area. A single segment of this species was found.

Pistacia atlantica var. *latifolia* is an Irano-Turanian element. It grows as solitary trees or in pure stands, or as an associate in maquis or forest of the *Quercus ithaburensis* association, in the Hula Plain, Upper and Lower Galilee, the Dan Valley and the upper Jordan Valley (Figure 14).

Pistacia palaestina is an East Mediterranean element. It grows as a tree or shrub in maquis and garigue, mainly on hills and mountains, in the Hula Plain, Upper and Lower Galilee, the Dan Valley and the Golan.

Pistacia vera is a steppe tree that does not grow wild in Israel. Its origin is the Irano-Turanian region, in semi-arid terrain, in Iran and adjacent countries.

Populus euphratica is an Irano-Turanian and Saharo-Arabian element, a tree growing on river banks and springs; in the upper and lower Jordan Valley it forms riverine forests, especially on the banks of the lower course of the Jordan River (Figure 11).

Pyrus syriaca is an East Mediterranean and West Irano-Turanian element. It grows as a tree in maquis and forests in Upper Galilee and on Mt. Hermon (Figure 10).

Quercus calliprinos is an East Mediterranean element, a tree or shrub in maquis and forest from sea level to 1500 m in Upper and Lower Galilee and on Mt. Hermon (Figure 14). It is the most common tree in Upper Galilee, where the annual precipitation is 500 mm and more.

Quercus ithaburensis is an East Mediterranean element, a tree growing up to 500–1000 m asl in the Dan Valley, Upper and Lower Galilee and in the Hula Plain, in small and scattered forest remnants (Figure 14).

Rhus. Three species grow nowadays in Israel. *Rhus tripartita* and *R. pentaphylla* cannot be distinguished by their wood anatomy. Neither grows in the vicinity of the excavations. *R. tripartita* is an Irano-Turanian element, a shrub, growing on rocks in deserts and among shrubs in the lower Jordan Valley. *R. pentaphylla* is a South Mediterranean element, a shrub or shrublet growing in Coastal Galilee and the Acco Plain. *R. coriaria*, a Mediterranean tree or shrub, is found today in neglected places near villages, rarely in maquis, in Upper Galilee and the Golan Heights. The specimens identified as *Rhus* do not fit the structure of *R. coriaria*, due to the presence of mostly septate fibres and the absence of spiral thickenings in vessels. The intraspecific anatomical variability may perhaps be greater than previously realized. On the other hand, the *Rhus* species identified here may be altogether different from the three species mentioned above.

Salix species cannot be distinguished by their wood anatomy. *S. acmophylla* and *S. alba* are trees that grow near water in the Hula Valley and Upper Galilee. *S. acmophylla* is an East Mediterranean and Irano-Turanian element and is more abundant than *S. alba* (Figure 11), a Mediterranean, Euro-Siberian and Irano-Turanian element.

Ulmus is a North and East Mediterranean element. It

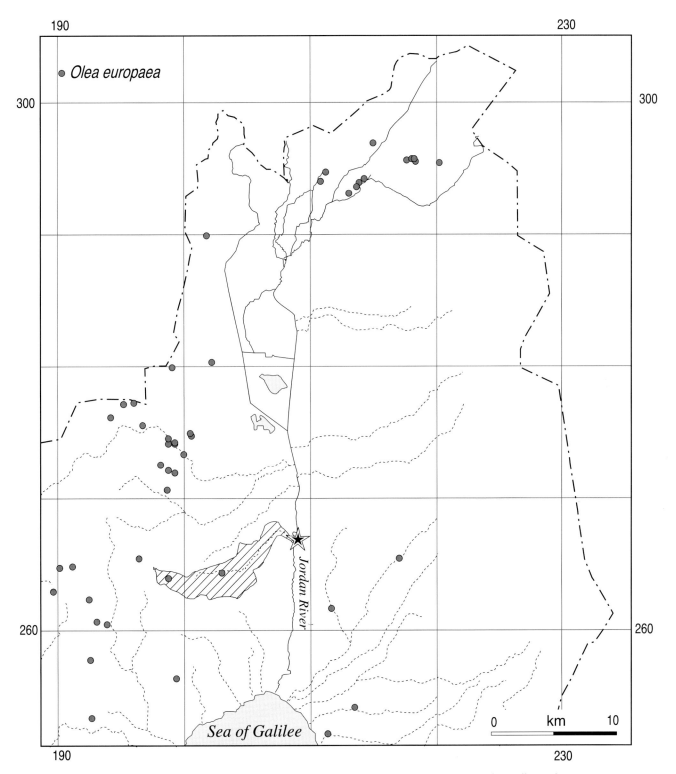

Figure 13: Distribution map of trees of *Olea europaea* growing in Galilee and the upper Jordan Valley today.

68

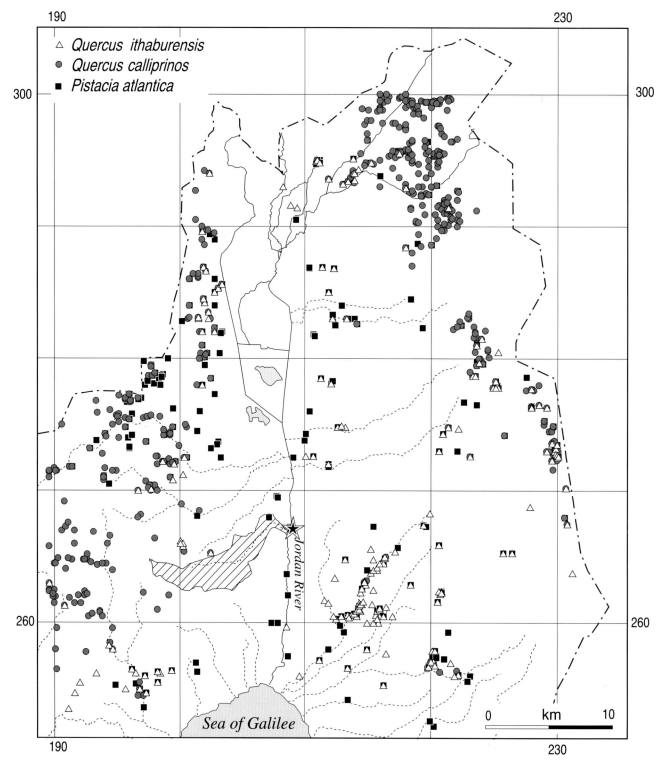

Figure 14: Distribution map of trees of *Quercus ithaburensis*, *Quercus calliprinos* and *Pistacia atlantica* growing in Galilee and the upper Jordan Valley today.

grows as a tree in shady places near water, in Galilee (Figure 15).

Vitis. The wild type of *Vitis vinifera*, *V. sylvestris*, is a climbing shrub growing in humid habitats such as riparian forests. It is an Euro-Siberian, Mediterranean and Irano-Turanian element. In Israel it occurs in gorges and in the vicinity of springs and streams along the upper Jordan River and its tributaries as well as in the Kinneret Valley (Kislev and Melamed, in press) (Figure 12).

Ziziphus/Paliurus. *Ziziphus lotus* is a Mediterranean and Sudanian element, a shrub growing in stony slopes and alluvial plains in Upper Galilee, the Dan Valley and the Golan. *Z. spina-christi* is a Mediterranean, Saharo-Arabian and West Irano-Turanian element, a tree growing in wadi beds and alluvial soils in Upper and Lower Galilee, the Dan Valley and the Golan (Figure 16). *Paliurus spina-christi* is a North and East Mediterranean and East Irano-Turanian element. It grows as a tree or shrub, mostly in alluvial soils, in Upper and Lower Galilee and the Dan Valley. The two genera, as well as the two species of *Ziziphus* which grow in Israel, cannot be distinguished unambiguously by their wood anatomy. Both species of *Ziziphus* are common today in the Hula Valley and on the Korazim basalts.

Unknown. Most specimens of the 'unknown tree' have quite well-preserved wood. Nevertheless, it could not be identified by comparison with available wood samples or consulting wood atlases, description of archaeological material from Northwest Europe, European Mediterranean countries and Egypt (Gale and Cutler, 2000) and the GUESS program of computerized database (except for a genus of the New World, *Bumelia* of the family Sapotaceae; Wheeler et al., 1986). This appears to be an extinct species at least in this region, not found in Europe, the Middle East or North Africa.

The species resembling in some features the wood anatomy of the 'unknown tree' are 1) *Retama raetam* var. *raetam*, a shrub that is a Saharo-Arabian element and whose nearest site of growth today is the upper and lower Jordan Valley, and 2) *Phillyrea latifolia*, a Mediterranean element growing as a shrub or tree in maquis and forest in Upper and Lower Galilee. It must be borne in mind,

however, that despite a similarity in certain anatomical features, a difference in even one feature may sometimes lead to remote families.

The Ancient Plant Communities
The GBY identified plants constitute several groups according to their habitats and their vicinity to the palaeo-Lake Hula, from water vegetation through bank vegetation to dryland vegetation.

Lake and marsh vegetation
Components of lake and marsh vegetation are not represented among the woody plant remains. This vegetation consists of herbaceous plants and various perennial, mostly monocotyledonous plants. The herbaceous plants generally have thin stems and roots, their tissues contain many thin-walled cells, and they are poorly preserved. The perennial monocotyledons may have thick stems, roots and sometimes leaves. However, these consist of a mixture of very hard and very soft tissues. Very hard vascular bundles, often accompanied by sclerenchymatous tissue consisting of lignified thick-walled narrow-lumened cells, are dispersed in a matrix of large, often thin-walled parenchyma cells that may be lignified or unlignified. The epidermis and some sub-epidermal layers may also consist of sclerenchymatous, very thick-walled cells that envelop the bulk of the parenchymatous cells with the vascular bundles. The large parenchymatous cells decompose easily and, though segments of the hard tissues may remain, they are small and thin and are easily missed, and even when found it is difficult to identify them taxonomically. Lake and marsh vegetation is extremely well-represented, however, among the fruit and seed remains (Melamed, 1997) and was certainly diverse and abundant at the site.

Bank vegetation
The following arboreal plant species from the assemblage grow near rivers and lakes: *Fraxinus syriaca*, *Salix* spp., *Populus euphratica*, *Ficus carica*, *Hedera helix*, *Myrtus communis* (though it also grows in maquis), *Nerium*

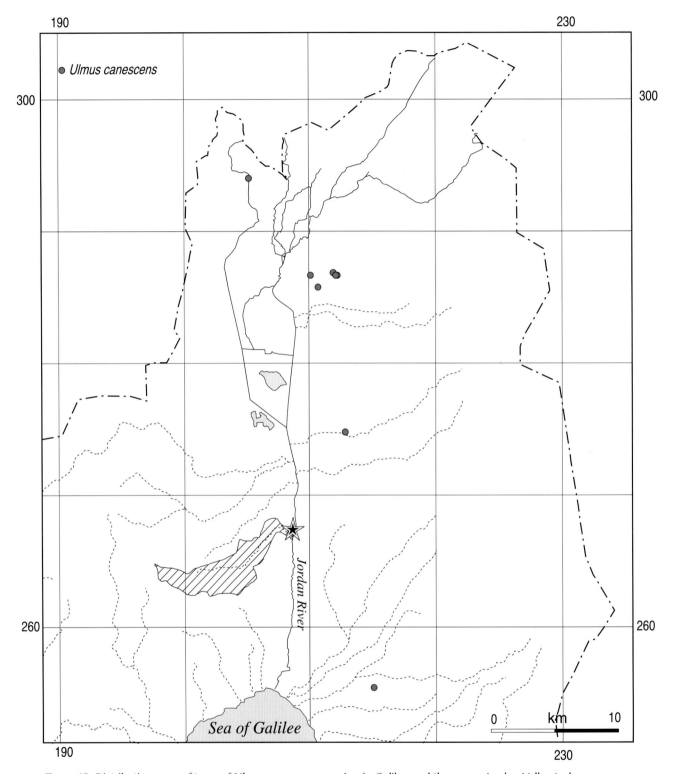

Figure 15: Distribution map of trees of *Ulmus canescens* growing in Galilee and the upper Jordan Valley today.

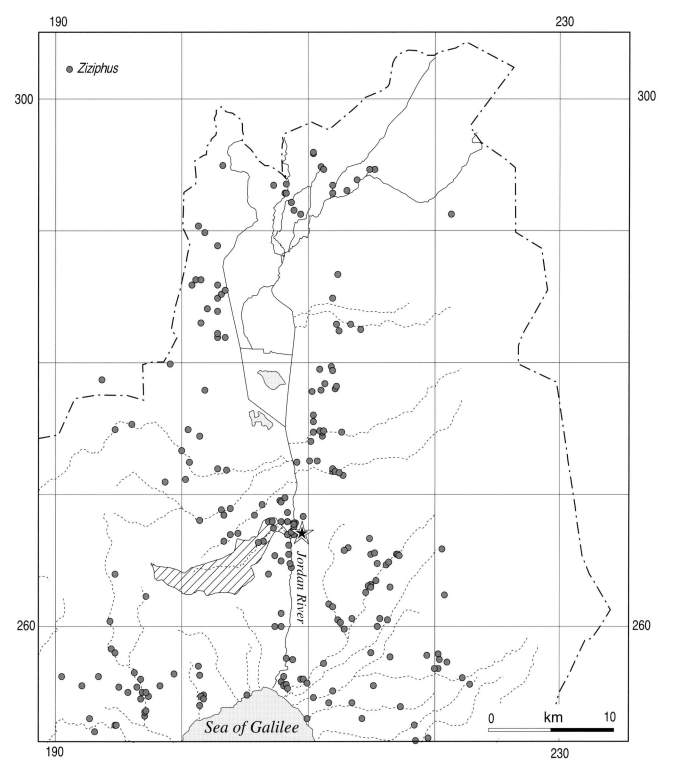

Figure 16: Distribution map of trees of *Ziziphus spina-christi* growing in Galilee and the upper Jordan Valley today.

oleander, *Ulmus canescens* and *Vitis* sp. All the above species also grow in the region today, though in different proportions from those found in the excavations. *Fraxinus syriaca* was found to be the most abundant plant species in the excavation (245 specimens), appearing in most layers except for those that are generally poor in woody material. The deepest layer in which it was found is II-7 and the highest V-5. In Layers II-2, II-5 and II-6, which have the highest total number of wood remains, those of *F. syriaca* compose one-third to one-half of the specimens (Tables 12, 13).

Ulmus canescens is represented in the excavations by 14 specimens in a smaller range of layers, the lowest being II-6 level 7 and the highest V-6. Both *Fraxinus syriaca* and *Ulmus canescens* are rare in the region today. Their relatively high percentage in the excavation, especially that of *Fraxinus syriaca*, further confirms the prevailing assumption that in the past these two species constituted the primary park forest in the Hula Valley (Zohary, 1959). Only remnants of that forest are found today.

Salix sp. is represented by 26 identified specimens and eight queried specimens, while *Populus euphratica* is recorded by only four examples; for two other specimens the two genera could not be differentiated. This can be explained by the fact that *Populus euphratica* is more salt tolerant than *Salix* sp. and is more abundant along the lower part of the Jordan River, while *Salix* sp. prevails in the northern part. *Salix* sp. specimens are found in almost all layers of Trench II (levels 1–7/8) and their highest appearances stratigraphically are in Layer I-5, Trench I and Layer V-5/6 (Table 14). *Salix* sp. is also common in the region today.

The three specimens of *Ficus carica* are found only in the upper part of the depositional sequence, in Layers II-2, V-5 and in Trench I.

The scarcity of climbers like *Vitis* sp. and *Hedera* sp. in the excavations, though both grow near water and despite the fact that many *Vitis* sp. seeds were found in the excavations (Kislev and Melamed, in press; Melamed, 1997), is most probably due to the fact that as climbers they possess relatively thin branches. The same may apply to *Myrtus* sp. and *Nerium* sp., which usually grow as shrubs.

Dryland vegetation

Other species grow further away, on different soils at various distances from the site of excavation. *Olea europaea* is next in frequency (45 specimens) to *Fraxinus*. The wild variety *O. sylvestris* grows mainly in the *Quercus calliprinos - Pistacia palaestina* association in the Upper Galilee and on the Golan. It is found nowadays not far from the Rosh Pinna forest and near Vered HaGalil between rocks where Eocene strata are exposed (not on basalt). Its wood was found from Layer II-6/7 upward (Table 14).

The two species of *Quercus*, *Q. ithaburensis* (26 specimens) and *Q. calliprinos* (27 specimens), are next in frequency to *Olea*. The first grows up to 500–1000 m asl and the second from sea level, but usually no less than 200 m asl, up to 1500 m. Remnant trees of *Quercus ithaburensis* are found nowadays in the valleys of the Dan and the Hula and those of *Q. calliprinos* occur not far from the Rosh Pinna forest. *Q. calliprinos* wood was found in the excavation from Layer II-7 upwards and that of *Q. ithaburensis* from as deep as II-12 (Table 14).

Due to the sometimes poor preservation of wood identified as *Quercus*, the two species *Q. ithaburensis* and *Q. boissieri* may have been confused, and a few *Q. boissieri* specimens may have been missed. *Q. boissieri* grows in forests and maquis, usually preferring higher altitudes or colder winters, in Upper and Lower Galilee (Zohary, 1966). *Q. ithaburensis*, *Q. libani* and *Q. cerris* do not differ anatomically. The latter two, however, do not grow further south than Mt. Hermon.

Myrtus communis, which, as mentioned above, is both a riverine and a garigue plant, is represented here by 7 (9?) specimens.

All the *Pistacia* specimens were found in Trench II. It is the only genus found in the lowest excavated layer in which wood was found (Layer II-14) and occurs up to Layer II-2/3 (Table 14). Thus *Quercus calliprinos* and *Pistacia atlantica* are the most ancient species excavated up to now. *Pistacia atlantica* accompanies the forest of *Quercus ithaburensis*.

Liphschitz (1990) claims that the primary vegetation of the Hula Valley was that of *Quercus calliprinos* and *Pistacia palaestina*. The large number of *Quercus ithaburensis* specimens, as well as those of *Pistacia atlantica*, refute Liphschitz's view, however, that *Q. ithaburensis* and *Pistacia atlantica* first appeared in the Golan Heights in the Hellenistic period.

The genus *Pistacia* has several well-defined anatomical characteristics by which it can be identified. However, within the genus interbreeding between species occurs, resulting in variability in the wood anatomy of the hybrids. Nevertheless, a key for identification of present-day *Pistacia* species which grow in the region, with the addition of *P. vera*, which does not, has been constructed (Fahn et al., 1986; Grundwag and Werker, 1976). The differences in wood characteristics between *P. atlantica* and *P. vera* are mainly quantitative. Therefore, one should be cautious in drawing conclusions on the basis of wood anatomy alone as to whether *P. vera* grew in the past in the GBY region. Different climatic conditions may have prevailed at the time and *P. vera* may have become extinct later on when conditions changed. Alternatively, the intraspecific variability in wood anatomy of *Pistacia atlantica* may be greater than has been observed up to now.

Only one specimen of *Pistacia palaestina*, consisting of a thin branch, was found. Since the anatomical characteristics of the first growth rings may differ from those of the following ones, this identification should be accepted with caution.

Three genera found in the excavation, though in very low numbers, grow nowadays in much drier regions: *Periploca graeca* (?), *Ziziphus* and *Lycium*. Only two *Ziziphus* specimens were found (in Layer II-6 levels 1 and 2) (Table 14), in contrast to its abundance nowadays on the border of the Hula Valley, owing to the devastation of the climax flora.

Despite the fact that certain species, like *Fraxinus*, grow on water banks, and others, like *Pistacia* and *Quercus*, on dryland but still in the Hula Valley, the anatomical sections of some of them exhibit series of very narrow growth rings including only earlywood. This is especially pronounced in ring-porous wood, where these narrow growth rings contain large vessels only of earlywood. This indicates either years of drought or some other types of stress (Photo 22).

Twelve 'unknown tree' samples were found in Trench II in Layers 2–7 and one in Trench VI, whose layers partly overlap the higher layers of Trench II. The wood anatomy characteristics of this species fit those of a dryland tree or shrub.

Chapter 5 – Wood Taphonomy

The aim of the present chapter is to acquire a better understanding of the mechanisms by which the wood segments were deposited on the shores of the palaeo-Lake Hula. These mechanisms are considered here as part of a taphonomic system since they relate to diverse processes that took place after the plants' death. The taphonomic analysis proposes several hypotheses. The acceptance or rejection of these hypotheses will be based on consideration of a number of variables. These include wood properties (taxonomy, size, spatial organization, etc.), stratigraphic and sedimentological context, and some of the processes operating in the ancient Hula Basin. It will also examine attributes that relate to the present geomorphology of the site's vicinity (fluvial systems, catchment areas and topography), as well as present-day climatological data, in order to attempt a reconstruction of the possible transportation modes of the wood.

Hypotheses

The prevalence of organic matter throughout the GBY sequence suggests that once it accumulated on the site preservation potential was extremely good, and that the critical biases in the wood record lie primarily in the mode of accumulation itself. None of the wood-bearing strata show evidence of well-developed soil formation and none of the wood specimens appear to reflect *in situ* growth (e.g. roots, upright position). Hence it is likely that all of the wood experienced transport to some degree before reaching the site. There are essentially three means by which wood segments could have accumulated at the site:

'The northern side is bordered by an extensive marsh, stretching in some parts quite across the whole valley, and covered with gigantic reeds and canes, through which the waters of the upper Jordan, lazily find their way.'

(Robinson, 1865: 180)

'…, it was perfectly clear that no boat or even a reed raft, or a plank, could get through the dense barrier before me. I much question whether a duck or at any rate a fat one, could go far into it, and only a fish would be safe…'.

(McGregor, 1870: 267-268)

'The whole marsh is marked in the maps as impassable, and most truly it is so. I never anywhere else have met with a swamp so vast and so utterly impenetrable. First there is an ordinary bog, which takes one up to the knees in water, then after half a mile, a belt of deeper swamp, where the yellow water-lily (*Nuphar lutea*, D. C.) flourishes. Then a belt of tall reeds; the open water covered with white water-lily (*Nymphaea alba*, L.), and beyond again an impenetrable wilderness …'.

(Tristram, 1876: 579-580)

1) They may have grown near the site and thus have experienced minimal transport prior to deposition;
2) They may have grown at some distance from the site and been transported to it by hydrological agents (e.g. by floating or traction in rivers or the lake);
3) They may have been collected by early hominins and brought to the site for a variety of purposes.

The first case represents a 'local flora' hypothesis, in which the components of the wood assemblage reflect local conditions near the site and contain no exotic elements. In this scenario, the ecological implications of the wood are directly related to conditions near the site. In the second case, the 'driftwood' hypothesis, the wood was introduced to the site by natural transportation agents and hence does not necessarily reflect local conditions at the site. The wood may have been assembled from a variety of points within the drainage basin and characteristics such as transportability, durability and size may have influenced both representation and abundance in the final sample. The 'hominin transport' hypothesis also places the origins of the wood at some distance from the site, but identifies hominins as the specific agents of transport. It implies some selection of wood for particular properties, such as burning quality, hardness or smell, etc. (Boyd, 1988). This hypothesis creates an expectation that the anatomical identification of the wood will reveal a dominance (archaeological concentration) of particular types of taxa in association with particular archaeological horizons/layers. The repetitive occurrence of wood, with over 1400 specimens in more than 25 stratigraphic levels, implies that the accumulations have a uniformitarian rather than a catastrophic explanation, though the exact processes may have varied through time.

Evidence

Various lines of evidence can be examined to test these hypotheses and determine which (individually or in combination) best account for the assemblage recovered from the site. This taphonomic assessment is critical for understanding the mode of accumulation of the wood, and ultimately how the wood evidence can be used to infer ancient plant communities and habitats for the Hula Valley.

Depositional context of wood at the site

The stratigraphic and sedimentological analyses of the GBY deposits indicate that the wood assemblages are an integral component of the deposits. Wood occurs in association with all of the major sedimentary facies (channel conglomerates, beach sands/coquinas, offshore muds) throughout the section. The regular pattern of wood in association with a wide range of lithologies, from muds to conglomerates, is in accordance with other evidence that the wood is not an *in situ* (i.e. in growth position) occurrence. Though most of the woods represented have strong substrate preferences, the taxonomic representation does not vary with sedimentary context. Some degree of transport to the site is clearly indicated.

Although the sample is biased by excavations that focused on the artefact-rich levels, there is a strong association of wood with the archaeological occurrences. A very close association between the wood items, the stone tools and animal bones was repeatedly observed. This was particularly evident in Layer II-6 level 1, where wood pieces were very abundant (Goren-Inbar et al., 1994). On this horizon (Figure 17), a wooden log was found in association with an elephant skull and many other lithic artefacts. The log was beneath the skull in a position that was interpreted as a result of hominin involvement. Other items of the same level appeared on

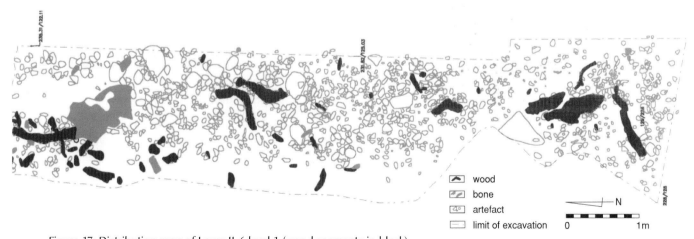

Figure 17: Distribution map of Layer II-6 level 1 (wood segments in black).

top of, together with, and below the wood segments. Further evidence for the primary depositional context of the wood is derived from the dense concentration (ca. 37,000) of stone artefacts smaller than 2 cm in this level. These were found in association with the log and the elephant skull (Goren-Inbar et al., 1994) (Photos 29, 30 below) and hence rule out the possibility of winnowing or other post-depositional processes. Additional support for the primary association of the wood pieces in Layer II-6 level 1 derives from the nature of the spatial associations encountered on the various horizons: for example, a large piece of wood that was found with basalt handaxes (Figure 18) and the association between several pieces of wood and stone artefacts in their proximity (ibid. and Photo 30). The depositional origin of Layer II-6 is that of a stacked, multi-component beach (Feibel et al., 1998; Feibel, 2001). The wood assemblage is thus an original component of these palaeo-lake shores and is contemporaneous with the other components of these

horizons. Although the sample is admittedly smaller, wood does occur in levels where few or no artefacts or bones were recorded.

Repetitive plant composition throughout the stratigraphic sequence

The taxonomic composition of the different assemblages throughout the history of deposition at the site (Tables 9–11) includes both *autochthonous* woods (growing near the site) and *allochthonous* woods (growing at a distance from the site) (for definition of terms see Spicer, 1989). The autochthonous species are composed of bank vegetation that grew on the lake shores or river banks and are present in assemblages due to bank erosion and/or death of plants. The allochthonous species are typical of dryland and higher elevations, e.g. mountainous terrain located at some distance from the palaeo-lake.

The autochthonous taxa in the GBY wood assemblages are dominated by a single bank plant species, *Fraxinus syriaca*, which exceeds by far the quantities of all other identified taxa. *Fraxinus syriaca* is accompanied by smaller numbers of many other species of bank vegetation, mainly *Salix* and *Ulmus*. This repetitive pattern can be accommodated in the first hypothesis outlined above, favouring a local origin of the wood, or may represent specimens derived from the banks of the drainages entering the lake. Allochthonous taxa include *Olea*, *Quercus* and *Pistacia*. The pattern of allochthonous vegetation, also repetitive, supports the second hypothesis relating to wood segments that were transported into the lake, floating in water until deposited on the shoreline or in the marginal swamps. Therefore, both the first and second hypotheses are supported by the overall assemblage.

The repetitive composition of the plant assemblages and their similar frequencies at different levels, as revealed in Tables 9–11, apply to all wood-bearing layers of the non-conglomerate depositional facies studied at the site, and reflect both high and low water-level stands of the palaeo-Lake Hula (Chapter 3). Any deviation from the natural processes would have caused a bias in this repetitive pattern, possibly resulting in augmentation of

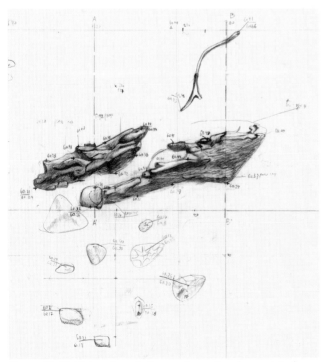

Figure 18: Field drawing of pieces of wood and associated stone artefacts (including handaxes).

one or more wood taxa growing at a distance from the lake, preferred and selected by hominins and not necessarily the same in each of the studied layers. The lack of such a bias in taxonomic representation indicates that the third hypothesis of hominin intervention is implausible, or at best of minor significance.

Size

Size (i.e. length, width or thickness), hardness and specific morphology, among other traits, could have been the focus of intentional and specific wood gathering/collecting effort by ancient hominins, but none of the above characteristics was observed to be dominant at the site. The hypothesis that hominins introduced wood into their sites on the basis of size must be ruled out, since most of the wood fragments excavated at GBY are very small (Table 15; Figure 19).

The lack of longer and thicker branches of wood supports the second hypothesis. Table 16 presents the size of the wood segments. Length is considered here as representative of the fragment's dimensions, since it strongly correlates with the other size attributes (width and thickness) as shown below (generated with Abacus Concepts, 1992). The possibility that twigs were collected for firewood (brushwood for feeding hearths) is also doubtful, as no hearths were exposed during the excavations. However, there are some indications for the presence of fire, which derive from both burnt flint and charcoal (see below). The presence of hearths was reported in 1952 (see Chapter 1 and Appendix 1) from a sector of the site which is located several hundred metres north of the present study area.

Tables 17 and 18 present a selection of data from selected layers and from selected levels of Layer II-6 respectively. They include only the largest samples that permit significant statistical analyses. In general, the mean size of wood segments is quite similar in all layers, with minor variations. Layer II-7 is characterized by the highest mean values, but also the highest standard deviations, and thus could be similar to the overall length distributions of

Table 15: Mean size values (cm) calculated for the entire measurable wood assemblage.

	mean	s.d.	N
Length	9.3	9.7	821
Width	3.2	2.8	817
Thickness	1.7	1.8	816

Table 16: Correlation matrix of wood segment dimensions.

	Length	Width	Thickness
Length	1.000	.679	.714
Width	.679	1.000	.810
Thickness	.714	.810	1.000

816 observations were used in this computation
48 cases were omitted due to missing values.

Table 17: Length statistics of wood segments from selected layers (cm).

Layer	Mean	s. d.	s. error	Min.	Max.	N
V-5+V-6	6.72	4.65	.76	0.60	21.40	37
II-2	9.52	8.58	1.04	3.00	41.00	68
II-5	8.11	7.61	1.05	3.00	45.00	53
II-6	8.33	9.91	0.49	1.50	111.00	414
II-7	13.58	12.23	2.35	3.00	45.00	27

Table 18: Length statistics of wood segments from selected levels[*] of Layer II-6 (cm).

Level	Mean	s. d.	s. error	Min.	Max.	N
II-6 level 1	11.93	15.34	1.28	1.60	111.0	144
II-6 level 2	7.49	4.32	0.49	1.60	21.50	77
II-6 level 4	5.75	3.65	0.54	2.00	18.70	46
II-6 level 7	6.07	3.63	0.36	2.00	21.00	101

[*] All the other levels have similar values, perhaps indicating similar conditions.

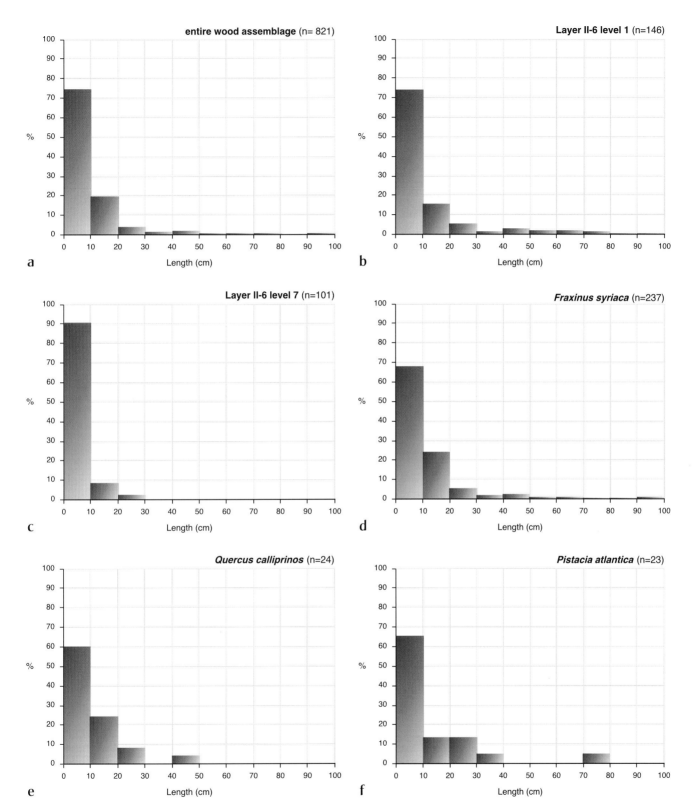

Figure 19: Length distribution of wood segments; a) entire assemblage; b) Layer II-6 level 1; c) Layer II-6 level 7; d) *Fraxinus syriaca*; e) *Quercus calliprinos*; f) *Pistacia atlantica.*

the other layers. Interestingly, the sample size does not affect the length values. The high standard deviations can be explained as typical of driftwood, where little size sorting occurs. The youngest layers in Table 17 (V-5 and V-6) are also the smallest in mean size and are more homogeneous in dimension.

When maximum values of all layers are examined, Layer II-6 stands out as the one with the longest pieces of wood. Table 18 presents the segment lengths according to the stratigraphic subdivision of Layer II-6. Layer II-6 level 1 is characterized by the largest wood fragments and by a large size spread. This phenomenon was observed during fieldwork and is reported elsewhere in this work. No other level of Layer II-6 matches it. It seems, as indicated above, that the transport of the wood to this layer 'documented' an event that was unparalleled, though not drastic enough to indicate a shift in the hydrographic regime.

The mean length of wood segments of the different species is presented in Table 19. The longest pieces are those of *Quercus calliprinos* and *Pistacia atlantica*, followed by *Fraxinus syriaca*. The bark pieces are the shortest and their standard deviations show a relatively small spread. A combination of two factors is probably responsible for the size of the segments:

1) Degree of hardness of the plant wood tissue. This depends on anatomical features such as wall thickness of fibres and other cell types, the relative amount of thin-walled parenchyma cells, the

frequency and diameter of vessels, the presence of spiral thickenings in vessels, the presence of dark materials in cells, etc.

2) The distance between the site of growth and the lake, and the specific location of the archaeological site.

Examples of the combination of these two factors are the following. The longest wood segments (Table 19) are those of *Quercus*, *Fraxinus* and *Pistacia*. This can be explained by the fact that *Quercus* and *Pistacia*, though they grow at a distance from the site of the excavations, have very hard wood. The wood of *Fraxinus* is less hard, but the tree grows on the water bank. The segments of *Salix* are relatively short; though *Salix* is also a water bank plant, its wood is soft.

A different, more specific factor which may also play a role in the size of segments is demonstrated by *Olea*, for example. Its wood is hard but the segments are relatively short. This may perhaps be due to the fact that, with time, its trunk becomes hollow in the centre, rendering it more breakable. Bark is usually softer than wood and tends to crumble.

Spatial organization

The spatial organization of wood pieces can be informative and indicative for the taphonomic analysis, revealing both the mechanism of deposition and characteristics of the environment of deposition. Useful spatial information is limited to the controlled excavations. This may contribute to a better and more precise understanding of the palaeogeography of the ancient lake and its shores. The alignment of a shore can be deduced from the parallel orientation of logs along it. As the excavations at GBY are characterized by a limited spatial exposure due to the pronounced tectonic tilting of the layers, the layers' deformation allows excavation along the strike but limits the exposure along the dip (see Chapter 2). Thus, it is only rarely, such as the case of Layer II-6 level 1 and its southern exposure in Layer VI-12, that the distribution of wood segments shows a repetitive pattern (Figure 17). The observed pattern enabled only a suggestion of the

Table 19: Length statistics of wood segments of selected species (cm).

Botanical identification	Mean	s. d.	s. error	Min.	Max.	N
Fraxinus syriaca	10.3	10.3	0.7	1.8	97.00	237
Olea europaea	8.9	4.8	0.7	2.5	20.2	42
Pistacia atlantica	13.5	12.9	2.7	3.5	70.00	23
Quercus calliprinos	14.7	22.2	4.4	1.5	111.0	25
Quercus ithaburensis	9.8	11.0	2.2	2.0	53.5	25
Salix	9.1	5.8	1.2	3.2	25.9	25
unknown tree	6.7	2.8	0.8	2.0	11.8	13
bark	5.2	4.1	0.4	2.0	39.0	96

Photo 23: A log in Layer II-12.

Photo 24: A log in Layer II-12.

orientation of the palaeo-shore, in this case an approximately north/south axis.

The wood items that have been excavated from the site's geological trenches do not contribute to the analysis of the palaeogeography of the lake. However, the wood pieces in the trenches' sections demonstrate that the occurrence of plant materials is not restricted to the Acheulian occupations. Their presence serves as an indication of the taphonomic origin of the wood, since segments also appear in layers devoid of lithic artefacts. Despite the evidence that some layers are richer in woody material than others, and that the finds reflect a particular environment of deposition, one should bear in mind the case of Layer II-12, in which the longest wooden log was excavated (Photos 23 and 24; Figure 20). During

excavation one minute, extremely fresh and sharp flint flake (11x15x6 mm; maximum length 16 mm) was exposed next to the log. This find raises the possibility that somewhere within this geological layer there was an Acheulian occupation, but Trench II was apparently placed at a distance from the unknown concentration of artefacts. Another possibility is that the single small flake was a 'drop', an isolated find unrelated to a spatially nearby occupation.

Another aspect of the spatial organization is concerned with the depositional orientation of the segments, unrelated to their length. Examination of all the excavated surfaces at GBY failed to reveal any of the stratification, superposition or imbrication of many pieces of wood that is so typical of lake-margin driftwood (Photo 25). A single

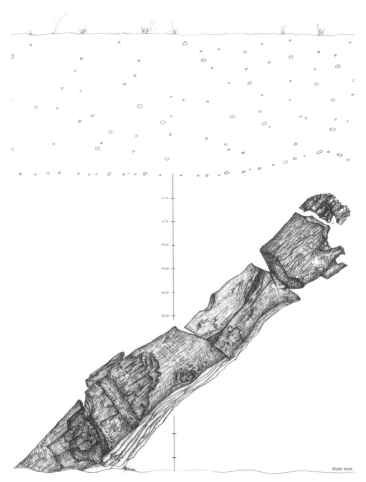

Figure 20: Log in the northern face of Trench II (Layer II–12; field drawing).

Photo 25: Typical accumulation of driftwood (photographed in North America).

case of one item on top of another was excavated in Layer II-6 level 1 (Figure 17). The lack of large accumulations of wood is not characteristic of driftwood and may indicate specific conditions of the ancient water body (low energy, lack of strong current, dense belt vegetation, etc.). On the other hand, it may relate to the nature of the bank vegetation, which should perhaps be reconstructed as not very dense (open park forest).

Summary

The evidence presented above demonstrates that the wood occurs as an integral component of all depositional facies, but that it is consistently transported rather than *in situ*

material. While the bank components of the assemblage may have derived from points near to the site, the regular representation of allochthonous forms demonstrates a persistent component of long-distance transport in the assemblages. Thus, the weight of the evidence points to the driftwood hypothesis as the best scenario for the origin of the GBY woods.

Models of Wood Transportation

Establishing the origin of the wood in the GBY strata as driftwood deriving from long or short distances enables us to proceed towards an attempt to reconstruct more of the palaeoenvironmental setting and of the mechanisms that transported and deposited the wood segments. To this end, models that may explain the presence and characteristics of the wood assemblage at GBY will be considered here.

One possible model views the wood at the site as the final depositional phase following transport by a normal fluvial agent or, in extreme cases, as a result of higher energy events such as flash floods. The latter result from heavy winter storms that occur at present in the Mediterranean zone, albeit rarely. Such storms can cause destruction of vegetation resulting from the heavy run-off of a rapid build-up of water, and the transport of substantial amounts of debris into the drainage system and through the fluvial system into the erosional basin. The process ends with the floating and later sinking of the wood on the lake shores.

At present, the Jordan River is the only perennial fluvial system south of the Hula Basin. Geological and morphotectonic research of the study area has indicated that this system did not exist during Pleistocene times (Belitzky, in press; n.d.). A model that requires a fluvial agent draining a catchment area characterized by marked differences in elevations will depend on the size, topography and lithology of the drainage basin.

A second alternative is a model of bank vegetation falling into an adjacent water body. The wood pieces float until they sink on the densely vegetated shores, analogous to those of the recent lake (Dimentman et al., 1992). This model is characterized by wood species that grow on the banks of the lake and is quite limited in the number of represented taxa, as the expected number of woody species along the shores is low. These two models should be integrated to formulate a single composite one. The reasoning behind this combination is the diversified habitats which are reflected in the identification of the different wood taxa of the GBY assemblage.

The Nature of the Wood Assemblage

Reconstruction of the origin, transportation and deposition, in addition to the botanical identification, of the wood segments excavated from GBY contributes much to the palaeoenvironmental reconstruction of the site and the adjacent regions.

The sedimentological analysis has assigned a mainly limnological origin to the deposits and favours an interpretation that views the sequence as reflecting a palaeo-lake shoreline environment from which the wood items were recovered. The small size of the wood segments (this chapter and Tables 15–19) and their scarcity in the archaeological horizons contribute additional data. The reconstruction attempt also relies on data on the site's palaeogeographical location (situated at some distance from a river confluence with the lake) and its relationship with the palaeo-Lake Hula. The sedimentological analysis indicates that the palaeo-river was not a high-energy one and therefore was not characterized by a turbulent water regime, at least in the close vicinity of the site. This is further supported by the results of the wood analysis, which failed to show the contribution of a fluvial system transporting and depositing the large wood pieces and/or clustered wood fragments that are typical of a high-energy regime. Moreover, several observations concerning the wood pieces should be added. The first is the horizontal position of the pieces. Except for an isolated case or two, the wood pieces were aligned with the depositional plane and not perpendicular to it. An extensive sediment contribution to the lake (i.e., fierce storms and floods) would have resulted in the build-up of a massive sedimentary unit including multioriented, imbricated wood items, stones etc. The driftwood observed today in the Jordan River is markedly different from that of the site and is indeed indicative of the high discharge and velocity typical of a fluvial system and not of a shallow lake. The situation consistently encountered at the site, which is typical of all levels, is that of an even and thinly scattered distribution of wood items lacking a single predominant orientation, e.g. Layer II-6 level 1 (Figure 17), Layer II-6 level 4 (Goren-Inbar and Saragusti, 1996). An additional observation is the absence of stumps with roots and leaf mats, which are considered markers of storms and other forms of catastrophic natural phenomena.

Thus, the small size of the wood segment, their scarcity

84

and the usual lack of predominant orientation are indicative of a lake littoral and conditions similar to those which prevailed in the recent shallow Lake Hula before it was drained.

The Origin of the Driftwood

At present the Jordan River is the only fluvial agent which can deposit driftwood at the site. The driftwood deposited by the river is characterized by higher energy than that documented at the site and is therefore not analogous to the Pleistocene system. Therefore, the reconstruction of the GBY palaeo-drainage basin should be based on postulating alternative ways to understand the palaeo-drainage of this area. These attempts should consider the entire extent of the palaeo-lake and its surrounding, and therefore all the drainage systems. These systems are the potential contributors of the driftwood to the GBY site. Such an attempt should also integrate data obtained by the many drillings carried out during the last 50 years in the Hula Basin (Belitzky, 1987; Inbar et al., 1989, and references therein).

The site is flanked on the east by the Golan Heights, where no large drainage systems have developed, and where the basalts of the Golan Heights rise from the base of the valley (ca. 60 m asl) to heights of over 500 m asl. This lack of erosional features rules out this direction as a source of the driftwood.

The possibility that the driftwood was transported over long distances in the lake itself is examined below from the botanical and limnological perspectives. The model which postulates transportation of driftwood from the northern parts of the lake (where perennial rivers exist today and from where the largest amount of water is carried into the basin) and across the lake to the southernmost margins encounters difficulties. There are indeed deeply incised fluvial systems which flow into the northern Hula Valley and could have transported much driftwood from different drainage areas. These fluvial systems could theoretically have transported all the representatives of the three-belt floral taxa encountered at the Acheulian site. However, this option must be rejected for three reasons: a) lakeshore

vegetation, b) depth of water, and c) pattern of the prevailing seasonal wind direction.

a) The Holocene Lake Hula, a shallow water body, is analogous to the Early/Middle Pleistocene lake due to similarities in the sedimentological composition and ecological conditions. Observations of the Holocene lake have demonstrated an extensive swampy area which was located north of the lake and covered a surface of ca. 130–190 hectares including the surface covered by water as a result of seasonal flooding (Dimentman et al., 1992; Karmon, 1956). The gradient of the swamp was minimal, in the order of 0.5 (Karmon, 1956: 16, 26). This area was extensively covered by a thick growth of papyrus (*Cyperus papyrus*) and rich organic material consisting of decomposed vegetation (peat/lignite). The swamps were drained by two river systems (the Jordan River on the west and the Tue'a to the east). If driftwood were carried by the water that originated north of the swamps (most of the Hula drainage catchment area is situated north of the lake and swamps), it would have had to cross all of the swampland before reaching the lake itself. Then it had to drift across the lake (from north to south) to be deposited in the southernmost area of the embayment. It seems likely that the dense swamp vegetation would have trapped it all. Even if there were strong enough currents along the shores of the palaeo-lake (despite its shallowness), a further obstacle would have been the typical shore/margin vegetation belts which would have trapped the wood (Dimentman et al., 1992, and figs. 7, 10, 12).

Long-distance transport across the swamps and lake should have resulted in a variety of taxa and sizes due to variation in the amplitude of the storms and the differing quantities and velocity of the in-flowing water. The homogeneity in the taxa encountered throughout the stratigraphic sequence points to relatively short-distance transport as well as a repetitive mechanism which contributed generally similar driftwood yields (taxonomically and in terms of size).

b) The Recent Lake Hula and its Pleistocene ancestor were both very shallow lakes. Strong and repetitive currents could not have developed in conditions where the mean water depth (as in the Recent lake) was in the order of 1.5–2.5 m with a maximum of 3–4 m (during winter) (Dimentman et al., 1992:18; Karmon, 1956).

c) According to Dimentman et al. (1992) the eastern shores of Lake Hula were strongly wave-battered, especially during the summer months, due to strong north-westerly afternoon winds. These winds winnowed a shoreline of coarser sediments (gravel, shells and coarse sand) and allowed less developed vegetation than that established in other parts of the lake. However, storms, which are also expressed in heavy rains and higher inflow of the rivers into the lake, occur only during the winter months. Figure 21 is a graphic illustration of the seasonal wind regime in the Hula Valley (as measured during three years at Kefar Blum, Hawwat HaHula). The wind roses clearly demonstrate that during January there is no dominant wind direction that could have been responsible for distributing the loads of driftwood which were introduced into the lake by the major rivers. Nor is development of a specifically oriented current responsible for the spatial arrangement of the driftwood along the shores of the lake.

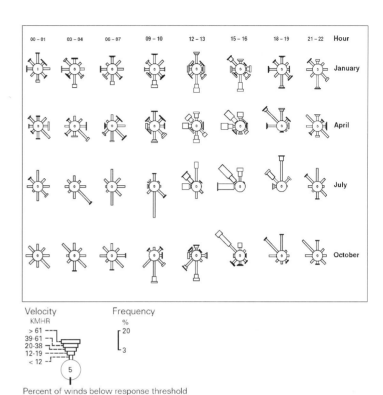

Figure 21: The seasonal wind regime in the Hula Valley (Kefar Blum, Hawwat HaHula).

The Proposed Model

Observations carried out beyond the Levant record: 'Isolated logs in non-marine settings, however, must have been growing within the drainage basin upstream of the point of deposition – a more or less definable area determined by the size of the channel complexes involved' (Spicer, 1991: 82).

Botanical and palaeoecological data resulting from the taxonomic identification of the GBY wood segments demonstrate that the wood species originated in different habitats and at different elevations. The agent responsible for the presence of driftwood at the vicinity of the site must be fluvial, for the following reasons: a) long-distance transportation in the lake is ruled out by the vegetation belts around it; b) the lake was characterized by shallow water and hence devoid of strong currents; c) the vast swamps located north of the lake would have blocked the driftwood from coming with the flows from the mountains.

One model for such a system is that of Nahal Rosh Pinna as a fluvial agent (Figure 22). Indeed, it cuts through both basaltic lava and sedimentary rocks (limestone and chert, some of which are of Eocene age) (Goren-Inbar et al., 1992a). It also drains quite an extensive range of elevations of the Safad Mountains, from ca. 900 m asl at the headwaters down to ca. 50 m asl at its confluence with the Jordan River. Nahal Rosh Pinnah currently joins the Jordan River south of the site. If this model is accepted (for details see Belitzky, n.d.; Feibel, 2001), the implication (based on morphotectonic and sedimentary considerations) is that during Lower/Middle Pleistocene times it flowed northwards. This model, due to the extensive difference of elevations within the Nahal Rosh Pinna catchment area, could fit the observed taxonomic variability of the GBY wood assemblages. However, certain species are extinct and do not grow today in the region. This model necessarily suggests that such plants as *Cedrus*,

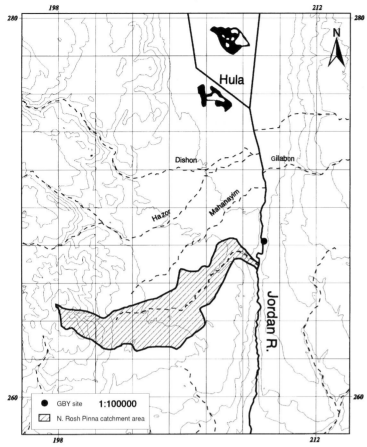

Figure 22: The catchment area of Nahal Rosh Pinna.

This would result in extensive geomorphologic changes within the catchment areas of these fluvial systems. The proposed model (Nahal Rosh Pinna) is geographically the closest system to the site, though the possible contributions of other contributing systems must be considered as well.

The identified wood taxa of GBY may be interpreted as representing three main floral belts reflecting different topographic elevations. These are the immediate lake/river bank vegetation like *Fraxinus syriaca*, *Salix*, *Ulmus* and accompanying shrubs and climbers, trees growing at higher elevations like *Quercus*, *Olea europaea* and *Pistacia*, and at the highest elevations, *Juniperus* and *Cedrus*.

Anatomical identifications of the wood from GBY demonstrate that the assemblage is comprised of elements that grow today at different altitudes. The wood assemblage includes a range of species, from those that grow in the valley where water is most available to trees growing at the highest elevations today (in the Lebanese Mountains: *Cedrus, Juniperus*). Species that occupy the middle ranges are common in the GBY assemblage and include *Quercus*, *Olea* and *Pistacia*.

Observations of the transportation distance of driftwood (logs) indicate that in many cases the distances are small and even minimal: '...the maximum distance this specimen ...could have travelled was only 1.5 km' (Spicer, 1991: 96). Spicer also wrote: 'The detritus from these distinct sources is mixed during fluvial transport over relatively short distances, and any resulting deposit provides a summary sample of the communities growing within the drainage basin' (Spicer and Wolfe, 1978). He further noted: 'Not all the communities are equally represented, however' (Spicer, 1989: 125). If indeed this is an analogous situation to the Pleistocene scenario of GBY, then the transport distance to the site is also a minimal one. Furthermore, this analogy may also explain the mixture of taxa originating in various habitats (topographies) that is present in the assemblage and described above. Thus, the presence of upland dryland taxa with those from lower elevations and from the Hula Valley itself necessitates a source that on the one hand was

Cerasus and the 'unknown tree' grew at the time in the region. Other models of neighbouring present-day rivers draining into the Hula Valley are clearly ancillary to that of Nahal Rosh Pinna and some of their catchment areas are at even higher elevations than that of Nahal Rosh Pinna.

The fluvial systems of Nahal Mahanaim, Nahal Hazor and Nahal Dishon are all options that may be considered as alternative/additional models for the fluvial agent responsible for carrying the driftwood into the Benot Ya'akov Formation. The difficulty in selecting a specific system stems from the great antiquity of the site and from the intensive and continuous tectonic activity documented in the region. Tectonic activity could easily have changed the flow direction of the rivers, a phenomenon responsible for the emphasized uplifting of the Korazim Saddle (Belitzky, 1987; in press; n.d.; Belitzky et al., 1991).

located near the site, and on the other also drained the highest elevations. The Rosh Pinna is the most suitable candidate for these requirements, as it drained a catchment area that was generally similar to the present one. Its ancient course could have deposited the *Cedrus, Juniperus, Olea europaea* and *Quercus* fragments in the palaeo-lake, together with and outnumbered by species representing bank vegetation such as *Fraxinus, Salix* and *Populus*.

A variety of other lines of evidence support an origin of the GBY wood assemblage within the Nahal Rosh Pinna drainage system. The southernmost exposure of the Benot Ya'akov Formation is located near the confluence of Nahal Rosh Pinna and the Jordan River. From the sedimentological characteristics of the exposures (lignite, different clays, *Viviparus apameae*) it is clear that the southernmost end of the palaeo-Lake Hula was located to the south of that of the Holocene lake, as the sediments here lack coarse clasts typical of the shores.

Three different lines of evidence support the model of Nahal Rosh Pinna as the source of the driftwood: a) the particle genesis of the sedimentary rocks; b) the structural and geomorphological characteristics of the site setting; and c) the chemical composition of the unmodified basaltic lava clasts excavated from the Acheulian horizons of the Benot Ya'akov Formation.

a) The sedimentological origin of the coarse-grained sediments in the study area is both allochthonous and autochthonous. They consist mainly of a component that is primarily basaltic in origin and may be derived from the immediate environs of the site (Feibel et al., 1998; Feibel, 2001; Goren-Inbar, n.d.). In addition, there is a minor component of limestone and chert that could originate only in the Safad Mountains located west of the site. The only analogous system that currently transports sedimentary rocks into the Jordan River is that of Nahal Rosh Pinna. As the eastern slopes of the Golan Heights in the vicinity of the site consist entirely of lavas, it is evident that the palaeo-Nahal Rosh Pinna was responsible for contributing sedimentary clasts in the range of cobble to sand-size into the GBY embayment. Until a few years ago, the palaeo-terraces of Nahal Rosh Pinna were visible and

comprised limestone and flint cobbles and pebbles, identical to those that were selected for artefact modification at the site (Photo 26). During extremely dry conditions (documented in the GBY composite section by conglomerates), the coarser clasts are indicative of a fluvial system flowing northwards and carrying a component of the above-mentioned sedimentary rocks (Feibel, 2001).

b) Analysis of the palaeo-drainage and morphotectonic evolution of the GBY area by Belitzky indicates that the present geographical configuration of the area has resulted from a long sequence of tectonic activity. He suggested the following sequence of events: '...the direction of the initial drainage net, which was formed in the

Photo 26: Limestone cobbles bedded in the Nahal Rosh Pinna terraces.

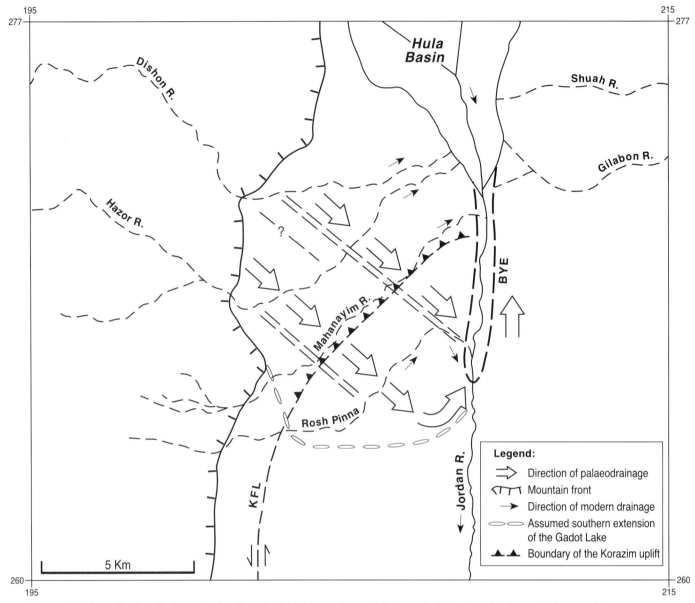

Figure 23: Map of palaeodrainage in the Korazim Saddle area (from Belitzky, n.d.; BYE - Benot Ya'aqov Embayment).

northern part of the Korazim Saddle after the cessation of the Gadot lake, was along the NW trending grabens. The fault controlled streams transported the Eocene and Cretaceous pebbles brought by Nahal Hazor (and probably by Nahal Dishon) into the GBY area. Subsequent uplift of the Korazim Saddle resulted in the formation of the Benot Ya'aqov embayment in which the sedimentary pebbles were deposited together with basaltic pebbles and boulders, apparently formed during the incision of the RPS (*Rosh Pinna Stream*). Fast subsidence of the Hula Valley Basin eventually caused capture of the NW directed stream segments to the NE, towards the subsiding basin' (Belitzky, n.d.) (Figures 23 and 24).

c) Geochemical analyses of basalt (Light, 2001)

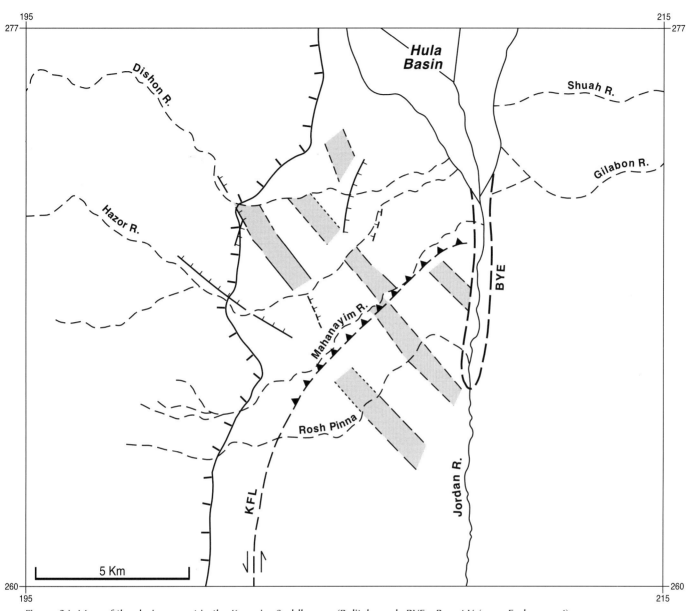

Figure 24: Map of the drainage net in the Korazim Saddle area (Belitzky, n.d.; BYE - Benot Ya'aqov Embayment).

documented similarities between basalt flows located south of the site on the Korazim Saddle (Belitzky, 1987) and a group of unmodified basalt cobbles and pebbles that were exposed and sampled from several archaeological occurrences at the site. The unmodified component (mainly pebbles) is smaller than the basalt pieces selected by the hominins for tool manufacture and

thus is viewed as a component of alluvial clasts deposited by a system flowing south-north.

The taphonomic analysis of the GBY wood assemblage provides two critical insights into the origins of this accumulation. First, the taxonomic composition and other characteristics of the assemblage indicate that the wood sample accumulated subsequent to transport as driftwood.

The accumulation process sampled at least three distinct altitudinally determined vegetation belts. The taxa best represented in the assemblages are bank forms, which have the highest likelihood of introduction to the transport system, but higher elevation and dryland forms are also consistently represented. A second result of the analysis is support of a model in which the Rosh Pinna drainage system was the primary avenue by which woods were derived from the different vegetation zones and reached the palaeo-Lake Hula system, eventually arriving at the shoreline setting preserved in the GBY site.

Chapter 6 – Wooden Artefacts

The recovery from the site of two wood specimens which were clearly utilized by early hominins (Belitzky et al., 1991; Goren-Inbar et al., 1994) marks GBY as the oldest known record of this relatively perishable component of material culture. In light of the unique nature of this record, the two specimens are described and discussed here.

The Polished Plank

A single segment of the GBY wood assemblage was identified as an artefact – a piece modified by the Acheulian hominins (Figure 25; Photos 27, 28). The segment was recovered from the waste dump of Trench II (Figure 2) and was assigned to Layer II-6 on stratigraphical and sedimentological grounds. The complete shape and morphology of this fragment is unknown, as the item was broken at both ends. It was discovered in 1989 and later described and published in detail (Belitzky et al., 1991).

The fragment is 25.0 cm long, 13.5 cm wide and 4.0 cm thick and is uncharred. The most striking feature is 'the single polished face... characterized by an extremely flat surface and by a slight convexity along one surface' (Belitzky et al., 1991: 351). Observed on this face were a single fissure and thin parallel striations, post-depositional features which probably resulted from the quarrying activities of Trench II. The polished plank was anatomically examined and found to be a fragment of a willow tree (*Salix*). The smooth surface of the plank is cut at a slight angle to the longitudinal radial plane of the branch as seen in transection. Clearly, exposure of the smooth surface is

unlikely to have occurred naturally at this angle (Belitzky et al., 1991: 352, fig. 2A).

Since the polished plank is unique, and as there are no other items of such antiquity that could be used as comparative material, the shape and function of the wooden plank remains unknown. Other European Lower Palaeolithic wood artefacts are all younger than the polished object, and most of them are very different in morphology: they are usually thinner, elongated items, spears of different kinds and dimensions (see below). Only one other item is described as a non-hunting artefact, an object of a 'tray' form, made of bark and thus differing in its properties from the GBY polished plank. This 'tray' was discovered in an Upper Acheulian horizon (Surface VI) at Kalambo Falls (Clark, 1969). The trough-shaped object is well preserved and measures 31x13x1.3 cm. Several similar but smaller items were also found at the same locality. The

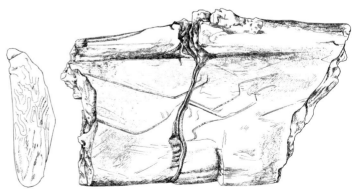

Figure 25: The wooden plank with polished surface: view of polished face and section.

Photo 27: Plan view of the wooden plank.

Photo 28: Section view of the wooden plank.

bark was identified as belonging to a Leguminosae tree (Whitmore, 1969: 221–224).

The Wooden Log

During the same field season (1989) excavations revealed a unique association of finds in Layer II-6 level 1. This association consists of an elephant skull (*Palaeoloxodon antiquus*), a basalt Levallois core, a basalt boulder-percussor and a wooden log (Figure 26, Photos 29–31). The finds and the association have been thoroughly discussed elsewhere (Goren-Inbar et al., 1994).

The log and associated items are integral components of the archaeological horizon, as explained in Chapter 5. It is one of the longest pieces of wood recovered in the excavations (longer items have been found in the walls of Trench II, but were only partially excavated due to logistical difficulties). The log is 106 cm long and 13 cm in diameter; it is slightly bent in the middle, its distal end is quite angular and it has many stumps of side branches (Goren-Inbar et al., 1994). The log was identified as Kermes oak (*Quercus calliprinos*). This oak has heavy, dense, strong and durable wood and its selection as an aid in the processing of the kill suits the foresight and planning revealed by other aspects of the material culture (e.g. the procurement of raw material, the reduction sequence of basalt knapping and those of limestone and flint). The following view of the

presence of the log within this group of finds was suggested: 'It is possible that the long, hard log may have been used as a lever, in order to manipulate the skull and turn it basal side up, the position in which it was later exposed' (Goren-Inbar et al., 1994: 108).

The log and the other artefacts in its close proximity were shown not to be a result of taphonomic processes but to reflect the original (or near original) spatial arrangement of the finds. The conjoinable elephant skull pieces, the thousands of tiny skull fragments and the tens of thousands of chips (basalt and flint artefacts smaller than 2 cm) surrounding the skull totally rule out the possibility that the log reached its final depositional locality by natural agents. The log was selected because of its length, strength and robusticity. The lateral growths were removed, though not by cutting.

The wooden log differs from long, thin wood pieces which have been reported from Europe and assigned to the Lower Palaeolithic of England (Clacton-on-Sea: Movius, 1950; Oakley et al., 1977) and Germany (Lehringen: Adam, 1951; Jacob-Friesen, 1956; Thieme and Veil, 1985 and Schöningen: Thieme, 1997). In contrast to the GBY log, the finds from these sites all bear clear marks of human involvement in the form of signs of modification (shaving, scraping, modification by fire and shaping a point) and all are thinner than the log. Moreover, despite

Photo 29: The wooden log *in situ.*

Photo 30: Flint artefact underlying the wooden log.

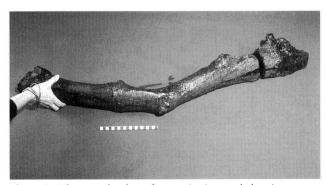

Photo 31: The wooden log after sectioning and cleaning.

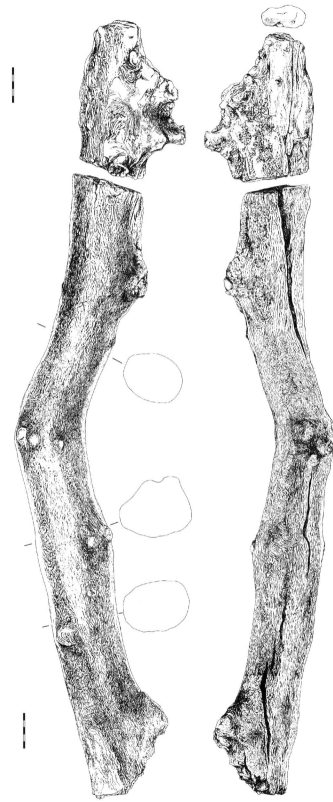

Figure 26: The wooden log.

the availability of many and varied sharp-edged artefacts in association with the log, no cutting marks or any other signs were observed on the log. It is clear that the function of the log from GBY differed from that of the spear-points found in Europe. However, the use of the log renders it a tool reflecting objective, function and accomplishment of the task. Planning is inherent in the capabilities of the hominins of these periods (Belfer-Cohen and Goren-Inbar, 1994), and thus the co-existence of two wooden 'artefacts' so very different from one another is not surprising.

Clearly, there is a need for additional studies beyond the results presented in this chapter. The focus should be on the identification of microscopic damage patterns that may be visible on the wood fragments, and on the spatial association of some of them. Moreover, the present study did not include experimental attempts to reproduce observed patterns, although this is viewed as an essential tool in order to achieve better understanding. A substantial effort was made to conserve all excavated fragments in a way that will enable their optimal preservation for future research.

Chapter 7 – Burned Wood

Since all of the wood segments were dark in colour, it was impossible to identify the burned items in the field, and it was only during attempts to section them for microscopic analysis that they were identified as being charred. Of the entire wood assemblage, 14 wood fragments were identified as burned. Table 20 presents the taxonomic identification, stratigraphic assignment, spatial location and size of each of the segments. Included in the table is an example of a specimen recovered from sieved baulk sediment. As the wood assemblage of the site includes only segments of 2 cm and larger (see Chapter 2), it should be taken into account that smaller items may have been present but not collected. It should also be noted that charcoal is more brittle than wood.

All the burned fragments were retrieved from layers in which lithic artefacts are abundant. An exception, to a certain extent, is Layer II-6 level 7, in which the sedimentological composition is slightly different from other levels and the burned pieces were found clustered in a sandy (crushed molluscs) channel fill, in which bands of dark organic material were observed to be interstratified (Photos 32 and 33).

Two possible explanations for the spatial clustering and relatively large number of burned wood segments in Layer II-6 level 7 (Table 13) were examined: the first considers this concentration to be a result of hominin activity and the second a result of natural processes. Some indications of fire, such as burned flint artefacts of various dimensions,

Table 20: Burned wood: identification, stratigraphic assignment, location and size.

Catalogue number	Botanical Identification	Layer	Square in Grid	Elevation (m)	L x W x T* (cm)
109		II–5	230/124	60.40	3.0x1.5x1.5
519	*Olea*	II–5	228/126	60.20/60.17	4.0x2.7x0.8
617	*Fraxinus* with bark	II-6 I 4b	231/124	59.69	3.7x1.4x1.7
818		II-6 I 7	234/123	60.02/60.00	2.3x1.1x0.6
834	*Olea*	II-6 I 2	229/127	60.29/60.27	4.4x0.9x0.7
852a		II-6 I 7	232/127	60.60–60.60/ 60.17–60.08	3.9x2.3x0.7
852a,b		II-6 I 7	232/127		
868f		VI–14			10.1x0.7x0.4
875	*Fraxinus?*	II-6 I 2	299/128	60.58/60.57	6.0x1.3x0.5
899a	*Olea?*	II-6 I 7	232/125	60.32	2.9x1.4x1.2
899b		II-6 I 7	232/125		
899c		II-6 I 7	232/125		
905	bark	II-6 I 7	231/126	60.22/60.17–59.74/59.70	4.6x1.9x1.3
sieved baulk sediment		II-6 I 4b			>2.0

* Length, width and thickness

Photo 32: Organic material in Layer II-6 level 7.

Photo 33: Organic material in Layer II-6 level 7.

were found in this level but analysis is still in progress. However, no additional indications of intentional fire such as hearths were found. The second option is based on the scenario that a brush fire occurred at some distance from the site and that the resulting charcoal pieces were transported by a fluvial agent into the drainage basin (the palaeo-Lake Hula). Spicer noted that charcoal floats easily and thus may be transported over long distances by fluvial processes (Spicer, 1991). However, due to the small

number of items originating in Layer II-6 level 7 it is impossible at present to relate these pieces securely to either the forces of nature or hominin activity.

The number of charcoal pieces from all other layers is small and precludes soundly based conclusions. Nevertheless, certain trends or suggestions may be noted. The expected frequency of burned material caused by brush fires should have been higher than that encountered at the site. If natural fire is ruled out as an overall explanation, then the presence of a small number of burned pieces could be interpreted as resulting from the use of fire by the occupants of the site. Other indications of burned flint derive from the presence of small chips (less than 2 cm), which were found in all the excavation areas. Preliminary investigations of flint chips from Area C demonstrate that there is a concentration (Layers V-5 and V-6) of burned pieces which seems to be the result of intentional activity involving fire (a hearth?). Although the locus itself was not exposed, the burnt flint chips reflect human activity rather than natural agents (concentration as opposed to high dispersal). It is hoped that these preliminary results will be supported by the extensive ongoing investigation, which may be very useful for supporting the notion that hominins controlled fire during Acheulian times at GBY. The very small size of the burned flint and wood pieces has parallels in much younger archaeological occupations such as the Mousterian (Stiner et al., 1995), in which small flint artefacts as well as burned bone fragments were encountered. This parallelism is partial; burned bone fragments are unidentifiable at GBY because of the dark patina cover so characteristic of the anaerobic environment of the waterlogged site.

The identified charcoal belongs to the two most abundant species, *Fraxinus syriaca* and *Olea europea*. The meagreness of the sample and the represented species will change in the future as a result of additional contributions of data derived from the analysis of burned seeds and fruits already reported from the GBY site by Melamed (1997).

Chapter 8 – Discussion

Plant remains are uncommon in archaeological contexts of Early/Middle Pleistocene age. Examples range from isolated and sporadic finds such as those of the Spanish Acheulian at Torralba and Ambrona (Howell, 1966) to the extensive samples of forests comprising thousands of logs, branches, fruits etc. originating from Kärlich, Germany (Gaudzinski, 1996). The particular conditions responsible for wood preservation may vary (Rowell and Barbour, 1990; Spicer, 1991), but centre on extremely dry or continuously wet conditions. Thus, wood remains are generally associated with particular post-depositional taphonomic processes, and may not directly reflect the original plant communities. The scarcity of such preservation conditions in eastern Mediterranean environments severely affects the potential for environmental reconstruction that depends on plant material. In view of this situation the presence of plant remains at GBY, and the wood described in this study, constitute a unique case that enables us to achieve a better understanding of both the palaeoenvironment and the hominin behavioural role within it.

This chapter presents a discussion of the results derived from the analyses described in the previous chapters. The aim of the wood investigation was to answer the following questions:

1) Where did the excavated wood segments come from and by what route?
2) Which taxa are present and what is their native habitat?
3) What was the palaeobotanical environment of the

'Having been directed to follow the Jordan to the lake Houle, we left Panias at 11 o'clock, and took that route. The beautifully wooded country did not continue for more than two miles, and we then entered into open rich plains. We found the ground very marshy: after wandering about to find fords over the numerous streams which water the plain, we crossed the Jordan itself, but the country on the other side was as full of marshes and swamps as that we had left, and in several places we nearly lost the horses…'.

(Irby and Mangles, 1844: 88; in February 24, 1818)

Hula Valley in the Early/Middle Pleistocene and how may this have affected hominin and faunal behaviour?

The conclusions reached here are restricted to the wood evidence. However, this investigation presents only one aspect of the multidisciplinary research work at the Acheulian site of GBY. It will definitely demand substantial reconsideration in the near future when the full range of botanical evidence is available, and their integration will undoubtedly create a rich and innovative botanical data set.

Lower Palaeolithic Wood Remains

When preservation conditions are suitable, wood and other types of organic material are present in archaeological sites, though this category of finds is usually very sporadic and rare. This scarcity precludes detailed palaeoenvironmental or behavioural reconstruction. Only in a few cases, and in special conditions, can the wood assemblage contribute much to the environmental reconstruction of a particular site.

Wood in the Levant

Pliocene wood and other plant remains older than the

earliest known archaeological sites are very scarce in the Levant. They usually appear as isolated items bedded in sedimentological sequences. The earliest case reported from Israel is assigned to the Pliocene Erq el-Ahmar Formation (Horowitz, 1979; Tchernov, 1973), located in the central Jordan Valley, where isolated waterlogged wood fragments were found and identified as *Fraxinus syriaca* (Braun, 1992). In the earliest deposits of the Lower Pleistocene 'Ubeidiya Formation (member Li), also located in the central Jordan Valley, several plants were identified (Lorch, 1966), including *Rhus tripartita* and *Pistacia lentiscus*. Chronologically, the wood remains of Gesher Benot Ya'aqov are younger. At Umm Qatafa Cave in the Judean Desert, in a later Acheulian context, well-preserved fruits of *Pistacia atlantica* were found preserved due to the extremely arid conditions in the Judean Desert region (Neuville, 1951).

Younger evidence derives from Middle Palaeolithic contexts, such as that of Kebara Cave, assigned to the Late Pleistocene (Baruch et al., 1992; Lev, 1992). This site yielded typical Levantine palaeobotanical assemblages, in which wood and plant remains are charred as a result of hominin activities in and around the site. The assemblages thus reflect intentional collection and gathering aimed at specific purposes (see also the Mousterian case of Douara Cave; Matsutani, 1987).

Wood beyond the Levant

In Africa south of the Sahara, the Early Stone Age site of Sterkfontein is one of the earliest to preserve fossil wood, dated to ca. 2.6–2.8 Ma (Bamford, 1999). The description of the botanical assemblages from the Acheulian site of Kalambo Falls yielded important information concerning the palaeoenvironment of the site and its vicinity (Chalk et al., 1969; Hodges and Clark, 1969; White, 1969; Whitmore, 1969; Clark, 2001). Further evidence of woody remains originate in the Acheulian-Fauresmith levels of Wonderwork Cave, South Africa, interestingly associated with indications of controlled fire (Beaumont, 1999).

In Europe, some of the earliest discoveries of fossil plant material were made at the Acheulian sites of Torralba and Ambrona, Spain. A variety of organic materials were exposed there during different excavations that were initiated in the beginning of the twentieth century and continued in the 1960s and subsequently (Biberson, 1968; planche V, b; Freeman, 1975; Howell, 1966; Echegaray and Freeman, 1998). The excavators reported the presence of wood, bark (only at Torralba) and wood casts in addition to a wealth of charcoal pieces. Other European Acheulian sites have also yielded data of plant material, due to the temperate climate and favourable preservation conditions that differ so drastically from those of the Levant. Such are the cases of Clacton-on-Sea (Bridgland et al., 1999), Bilzingsleben (Mania, 1988) and Schöningen (Thieme, 1997). The Lower Palaeolithic site of Kärlich-Seeufer (Gaudzinski, 1996; Gaudzinski et al., 1996) has contributed a wealth of palaeoenvironmental information based on 12,000 wood fragments (Gaudzinski, 1999). The interpretation of this wood assemblage, as presented by Gaudzinski (ibid.) and in contrast to previous interpretations, indicates a taphonomic process of a driftwood mass unrelated to hominin activities at the site.

Driftwood in Israel

The scarcity of lakes in Israel, the drainage activities that turned Lake Hula into agricultural land and the presence of fewer than five perennial rivers in the entire country contribute very few local data on the driftwood phenomenon. A limited description is given in the works of Klein on the Dead Sea (Klein, 1961; 1982), in which the author observed: 'All along the shore of the Dead Sea there is an almost uninterrupted belt of driftwood covered recent bars' (Klein, 1961: 7). Though the location, elevation, etc. are described, no details are given about the origin, size or taxonomy of the wood pieces. The nineteenth-century historical data cited (Klein, 1961: 29–53) refer to the possible origin of the wood and give some notes on the fragments' size, though these were only casual observations. Included are references to the '...largest trunks which I saw in Palestine... ' (Oline 1840: 67, cited by Klein, 1961), long logs and shrubs, branches, thorns etc. Based on observations made in 1867 (by Warren) and

1903 (by Mastermann) in the Dead Sea area, where driftwood covered an old shoreline that no longer existed during Klein's fieldwork, Klein concluded that driftwood may be expected to survive some 100–150 years on a shoreline. Evidently, limnological and fluvial processes induced by the prevailing climatic and environmental conditions are the major agents responsible for the durability of driftwood. The case of the Dead Sea driftwood cannot be considered analogous to the waterlogged wood segments found at GBY, where immediate sealing by waterlogged anoxic sediments enabled long-term preservation of the wood segments in the Benot Ya'akov Formation.

The Vegetation of the Lower Palaeolithic Site of GBY

The vegetation at GBY consisted of both woody and herbaceous plants. However, in most cases only plant parts that possess thick durable cell walls can, under the right conditions, be preserved for long periods. Such plant parts are mainly: a) pollen grains; b) seeds and fruits; c) phytoliths; and d) wood. The representation of these plant types, as well as the distance of their site of growth from the excavation, differ between the groups. Pollen grains have microscopic dimensions and represent both woody and herbaceous plants. They are usually surrounded by a very hard durable cell wall of which the external layer is principally composed of a highly resistant component, sporopollenin. In the absence of oxidizing conditions, pollen grains can be well preserved. However, they may be carried over great distances due to their microscopic dimensions. Seeds and fruits also represent both woody and herbaceous plants. However, they are either hard-coated, with lignin or other materials impregnating the cell walls, or soft-coated, and therefore can be preserved to differing degrees. They can be large or small. Therefore, they may be variously represented and dispersed over different distances. Phytoliths are crystal bodies found in various tissues of certain plant taxa, but the formation of some may be affected by environmental conditions and other factors (Warnock, 1998, 162, and

literature therein). Wood generally has relatively thick, lignified cell walls, though the thickness of the walls and the degree of their lignification vary between species. Wood, however, represents only woody plants, while small shrubs and herbaceous plants are generally not represented. In contrast to the three plant parts mentioned above, which are small or minute and easily become detached from the mother plant (especially the first two), woody organs are large (trunks, branches and roots) and rooted to the ground. Therefore, trunks and branches are often found *in situ* if not transported by water or storms, or by man (Nadel and Werker, 1999). Each of the above groups, therefore, can provide a certain limited type of information. Clearly, any attempt to reconstruct the palaeoenvironment and behaviour of Acheulian hominins in a specific terrain should be based on the integration of data from all types of assemblages. However, the analysis of other plant remains (pollen, seeds, fruit, phytoliths) from GBY is as yet in its preliminary stages. In view of the informative differences between the above types of assemblages, it was decided to present here the results attained thus far, in full awareness of the partial nature of the data.

From the perspective of vegetation, since the Lower/Middle Pleistocene transition 780,000 years ago the Hula Valley has had a Mediterranean vegetation. In Recent times, however, it has undergone a drastic change induced by human activity. Lush vegetation of the lake shores and swamps, as well as park or closed forest on dryland, existed in the past. It could sustain many large wild animals, some as large as elephants, rhinos and hippos. Today, due to the intervention of man, the lake and swamps have been drained, leaving only a small nature reserve of two lakes. As a result, there is increased dryland that consists of cultivated and waste places. These are accompanied by the scattered trees that are remnants of the past vegetation, with the intrusion of some late newcomer species resulting from this change, such as the shrubs of *Prosopis farcta* (a West Irano-Turanian element with extensions into Mediterranean territories) and, on the border of the valley, *Ziziphus spina-christi* (a Sudanian element with extensions into warmer parts of

Mediterranean territories) and *Z. lotus* (a Mediterranean and Sudanian element) (Dimentman et al., 1992; Zohary and Orshansky, 1947). In addition, there are some cultivated species planted by man.

The greatest change between the diverse taxa of the Pleistocene as represented by the wood assemblages of GBY and the arboreal vegetation of today is quantitative. This is most apparent in the small number of specimens of the bank vegetation *Fraxinus syriaca*, *Salix* and *Ulmus* today. It can also be seen in the scattered dryland trees *Quercus ithaburensis* and *Pistacia atlantica* today, in contrast to the large number of specimens of these genera found in the GBY excavations. Similarly, the number of trees of the wild variety of *Olea europaea* is greatly diminished.

Among the bank vegetation, *Fraxinus syriaca* (which has the largest number of specimens in the GBY wood assemblage) is known from the Pliocene (Braun, 1992), Upper Pleistocene (Liphschitz and Nadel, 1997) and many other archaeological sites located in the Dead Sea Rift such as Jericho (Liphschitz, 1986). It apparently constituted an important component of a bank forest. A present-day distribution map of *Fraxinus syriaca* (Figure 11) demonstrates the scarcity of trees of this species in the vicinity of the Hula Basin. At present, the closest known small group of *Fraxinus* trees grows in the Hula Nature Reserve, and farther away it is concentrated mainly in the Dan Valley, an evident marker of the destructive impact of modern forces on the natural environment. Since *Ulmus canescens* grows today only in humid and temperate regions of Galilee and Samaria, it has been suggested by Zohary (1982) that it is probably a relic of a rainier period. The presence of a relatively large number of *Quercus ithaburensis* and *Pistacia atlantica* wood segments in the excavations, and the scarcity of these species nowadays in the Hula and Dan Valleys, confirms the view of Zohary that these species represent a continuation of the Golan forest which once extended down to the valley (Zohary, 1959; Zohary and Orshansky, 1947).

Some changes in the vegetation, however, are of a more qualitative nature. *Cedrus* and *Cerasus* have never been known to grow in Israel. The ecological setting for the growth of *Cedrus*, as noted by Lev-Yadun (Lev-Yadun et al., 1996), is not found in Israel today. Both *Cedrus* and *Cerasus* grow nowadays in relic stands in the mountains of Lebanon. As noted above for driftwood (Chapter 5), the wood of these genera could not have drifted to the Hula Valley from the north, i.e. from Lebanon. A somewhat colder climate apparently prevailed in the region in Early/Middle Pleistocene times, and trees of *Cedrus* could have grown on mountains west of the Hula. It is worth noting that anatomical examination of the *Cedrus* segments showed, in addition to typical traumatic resin ducts, a zigzag twisting of growth rings (Plate 10A), both indicating some kind of stress during the trees' growth.

The occurrence of *Cedrus* is restricted to the uppermost limnic deposition cycle (Layers V-5, V-5/6 and V-6) in Area C, where it is underrepresented (2 segments). Therefore, it is impossible to conclude at the present stage whether these rare segments represent a change in the plant coverage during the deposition of the layers in which the segments were found, or whether it reflects a bias induced by methodological constraints (the minimal surface excavated). Interestingly, preliminary results of pollen analysis show very high frequencies of *Cedrus* pollen grains in the same layers as those in which the wood segments were found (Baruch, per. comm. 2000).

A similar argument for a colder period may apply to *Juniperus oxycedrus*, which grows in Galilee today but is rare. It is also worth noting that specimens identified here as *Lonicera* could be identified with species growing in Europe rather than with *Lonicera etrusca*, which grows in the region today.

On the other hand, 13 segments found in different levels could not be identified with European or Mediterranean species. The search for identification should perhaps be continued among more southern African arboreal plants or in the Far East. It must be mentioned that the wood anatomy of this unknown species fits that of a species from the New World, *Bumelia* of the Sapotaceae, a family that has no representatives among the wild flora of Israel. At this stage final conclusions on the causes of the qualitative changes in the vegetation since the Pleistocene are still premature.

Comparison between Finds of Wood and those of Seeds and Fruits

A total of 27 genera of trees, shrubs and woody climbers were identified in the wood assemblage of GBY. Six plant genera have been identified to date both by wood anatomy, as described here, and by seeds or fruits (Kislev and Melamed, in press; Melamed, 1997): *Vitis*, *Olea europaea*, *Pistacia atlantica*, *Quercus*, *Ziziphus*, *Ficus carica*. The fruits of all these species are edible (see below). The small number of wood specimens identified as *Vitis* may be due to the plant being a climber, with relatively thin branches.

When the species identified so far from seeds and fruits (Melamed, 1997) are compared with those from wood, two discrepancies are noticeable: a) the absence among the wood segments of *Styrax officinalis*, which grows nowadays in Upper and Lower Galilee (Figure 27), and its abundance among fruits; and b) the absence of fruits or seeds of *Fraxinus*, while this was the most abundant species among the wood. Since much of the fruit and seed material awaits identification, it is too early to understand the causes of these inconsistencies.

There is of course a great difference between the number of fruits and seeds found in the excavations and the number of the wood segments. Generally, one plant produces a very large number of fruits. Moreover, the greater variability of species represented by fruits and seeds identified up to now results from the fact that fruits or seeds usually become detached from the mother plant and some of them are dispersed over various distances by different agents such as wind, water or animals, while branches and trunks are rooted in the soil.

As noted above, only after completion of the research on seeds and fruits and on pollen excavated at the site will integration of all the palaeobotanical information be possible, and a full reconstruction of the palaeo-vegetation of the Hula Valley and adjacent regions accomplished.

Arboreal Plants with Edible Fruits

Different parts of plants may be used for various purposes. Fruits and seeds are usually consumed as food but may also serve many other purposes, for instance as spices or in a medicinal role, or, in the case of *Styrax* fruits, as a poison for fish. Wood, on the other hand, is more often used for tools, worked or unworked. This depends on various qualities of the wood, such as strength (like the large branch of oak associated with the elephant's skull), resiliency, ease of carving, etc.

Of the arboreal plants identified by their wood at GBY, the following genera have edible fruits or seeds: *Amygdalus korschinskii*, *Cerasus* sp., *Crataegus* sp., *Ficus carica* (Photo 34), *Olea europaea* (Photo 35), *Pistacia* sp., *Pyrus* sp., *Quercus* sp., *Vitis* sp. (Photos 36, 37) and *Ziziphus* sp. This number of ten taxa with edible fruits, out of a total of 27 identified taxa, is very high. Fruits of *Olea*, *Quercus*, *Pistacia*, *Ziziphus*, *Ficus* and *Vitis* from the excavation were identified by Melamed (1997). This high correlation between wood and fruits/seeds in the GBY excavations may result from various factors. The fruit-bearing trees may have grown in the vicinity of the site, hominins may have brought fruit-bearing branches to the site and picked the fruits there, or both fruits or seeds and wood were brought to the site independently because of their different potentials for use. All these possibilities may have occurred.

The three wood specimens of *Ficus carica* were found in the upper part of the section, in Layers II-2, V-5 and Trench I. Several akenes, however, were found by Melamed slightly lower in the section: one in II-9, two in II-7 and one in II-5 (Melamed, 1997). Due to the small number of specimens of both types of plant organs, no conclusions can yet be drawn from these data. Three woody plants with edible fruits identified here were apparently the origin of the cultivated species, i.e. *Vitis sylvestris* (Kislev and Melamed, in press), *Olea europaea* var. *sylvestris* (Feinbrun-Dothan, 1978; Zohary and Spiegel-Roy, 1975) and *Ficus carica* var *caprificus* (Zohary, 1966, 1980).

The edible arboreal plants represent only a fraction of

104

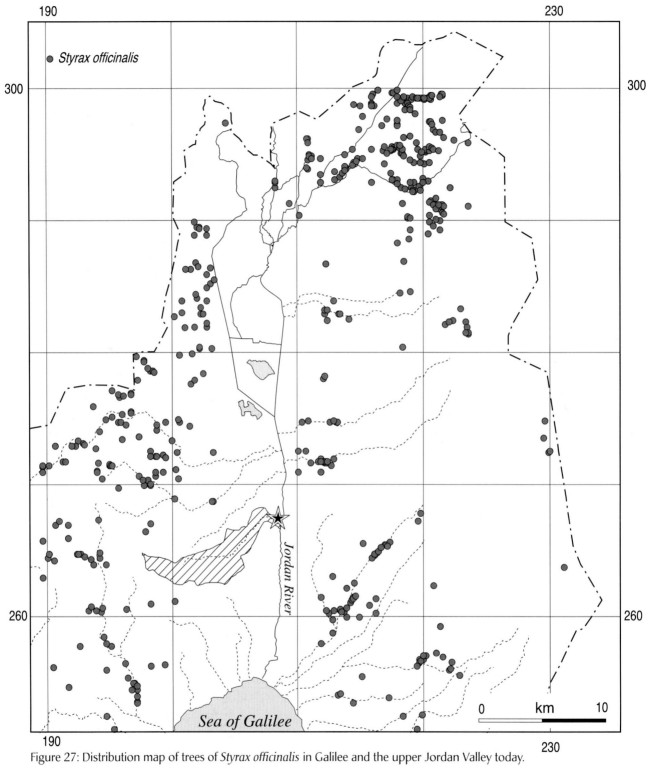

Figure 27: Distribution map of trees of *Styrax officinalis* in Galilee and the upper Jordan Valley today.

Photo 34: *Ficus carica.*

Photo 35: *Olea europaea.*

the total number of plant taxa with edible parts in the region, as identified according to their fruits and seeds by Melamed (1997). Edible parts of trees, together with small shrubs and a great variety of herbaceous plants, could provide a variety of opportunities for food throughout the year (see Rabinovitch-Vin, 1977) for both hominins and herbivorous animals. It can be concluded that the ecosystem of the upper Jordan Valley had an enormously rich potential for hominin subsistence. Patterns of exploitation during the Lower/Middle Pleistocene are a topic that can now be discussed for the first time.

The Scarcity of Wooden Artefacts

Hominin interaction with the environment, as expressed in the modification of wood artefacts found in archaeological sites, is minimal. Even in sites where wood preservation is excellent and abundant (i.e., Gaudzinski, 1996; Gaudzinski et al., 1996), wooden artefacts are usually absent or minimally represented.

Opinions on the presence of modified wood items from the sites of Torralba and Ambrona differ, some postulating human intervention and others refuting it (Biberson, 1968; Freeman, 1975). In the sites of Clacton-on-Sea (McNabb, 1989; Movius, 1950; Oakley et al., 1977),

Photo 36: *Vitis*.

Photo 37: *Vitis*.

Lehringen (Movius, 1950; Thieme and Veil, 1985) and Schöningen (Thieme, 1996; 1997; 1999), wooden hunting tools were found, all pointed and elongated, varying in wood species and dimensions. The small number of these artefacts (see also in Tydesley and Bahn, 1983; Bar-Yosef, 1997) cannot be explained by preservation conditions, since in some of the sites other types of organic materials have been preserved in large quantities. This scenario is similar to that encountered at GBY, where only a single wooden artifact, a polished plank of willow, has been found (Belitzky et al., 1991), differing drastically from the European tools. A somewhat analogous example derives from the Lower Palaeolithic Acheulian site of Amanzi Springs, South Africa, where wood material of different degrees of preservation was excavated from a spring pool and was interpreted as driftwood (Deacon, 1970: 116; Wells, 1970). This assemblage includes a single piece of wood which was exposed in Area 2 from the Deep Sounding, between Surfaces 1 and 2 (Deacon, 1970: Plate 15): 'This is the only piece of wood found in the excavation which showed any features which might evidence working' (Deacon, 1970: 152). Other isolated African artefacts are those excavated from the Acheulian site of Kalambo Falls, where a bark artefact was found. It has been previously described in this study (Chapter 6). Of the rich assemblage found at Kalambo Falls, Clark also refers to two worked items: a wooden club and a '…smoothed and pointed implement…' (Clark, 1970: 286, ill. 16). Recently, the wooden artefacts from Kalambo Falls were thoroughly described and illustrated (Clark, 2001: 481–491). An additional unique wooden artefact excavated in North Africa at the site of the palaeo-Lake Karâr in Algeria was an artificially notched log (Boule, 1900).

The minimal number of wooden artefacts in Lower Palaeolithic sites (and not only there) may have resulted from various factors.

1) All wood parts, unworked as well as artefacts, were broken into small pieces.

2) The lack of plant artefacts reflects the hominins' preference for the use of stone artefacts; such a hypothesis, however, contradicts ethnographic evidence drawn from present day hunter-gatherer communities, in which the stone artefacts are clearly the least common in the repertoire.

3) This perhaps reflects the relatively small lateral exposure (in sq. m.) at some of the sites, or excavations located beyond specific activity-areas that might have yielded more wooden tools.

4) Artefacts were made of plant material more perishable than wood. Even in sites where plant material preservation is good and where excavations yielded rich palaeobotanical assemblages, they do not necessarily reflect the original quantities of perishables. These instances are due to differential decay processes of plant tissues of various plant organs (see Chapter 4 for a detailed anatomical explanation). The vegetation belts that surrounded the Hula Lake were predominantly composed of reeds of various species (Dimentman et al., 1992). Of this wealth of plants, which undoubtedly also surrounded the Pleistocene lake, there is hardly any evidence, apart from fruits and seeds (Melamed, 1997) and pollen (Baruch and Bottema, 1999). A model explaining similar selective decay processes derives from a recent botanical study of the central Jordan Valley, from the banks of Lake Kinneret, described by Gafny (1992). Gafny's explanation of the deterioration and decomposition of tons of plant material is viewed here as an analogy to the situation that may have prevailed at GBY in antiquity.

The paucity of organic artefacts made of various parts of reeds and other plant material may be explained in the following way. Different data sets from GBY yield indications that the hominins carried/transported objects into the site (Light, 2001; Light et al., 1999). Hominin activities took place on the shores of the lake, where lush submergent and bank vegetation was available. They most probably exploited the local vegetation to facilitate the transporting of diverse objects and materials. Though processed reeds and bark components are absent from the GBY wood archaeological record, it is very likely that the technological sophistication so well documented in other aspects of the assemblages also included basketry and other forms of plant fibre usage as well as that of branches and twigs. Of interest is the observation made in 1894 by Worthington: 'the butt end when first found wrapped round with herbaceous stems, probably rushes, as if for protection of the hand' (in Tydesley and Bahn, 1983: 55).

Large basalt boulders and blocks were transported by the hominins to the site for the purpose of stone knapping that was aimed at the production of bifaces (handaxes and cleavers). Some of these archaeological pieces weigh over 15 kg and were undoubtedly much bigger before flaking (Goren-Inbar, n.d.; Goren-Inbar et al., 1994). In addition to these, it is now evident that some of the bifaces were introduced as *préforms* (roughouts), after being quarried from specific localities in the vicinity of the site (Light, 2001). All these were carried and placed on the shores of the lake.

The following is a possibly analogous ethnographic example that may throw light on the finds from the site and serve as a possible model. The meticulous ethnographic work of Pétrequin and Pétrequin on the stone axes of Irian Jaya in Indonesia (Pétrequin and Pétrequin, 1993) describes the mode of quarrying, transporting and later modification of the stone axes. A component of this system is the transportation of the *préforms*. These objects are carried in various ways including wrapping and tying with strings (Pétrequin and Pétrequin, 1993: 115, photo 94; p. 124, photo 101). Unfortunately, no such strings, worked bark or other organic materials were preserved at the GBY site.

Isolated, unique and rare finds are frequently evaluated critically and lead to discussions far beyond the realm of the organic materials. In the eyes of some scholars, this may be the case for the GBY Acheulian polished wooden tool, as it is intriguing by its mere rarity. However, the excellent state of preservation of this piece and its unusual characteristics contrast with those of all the other wood segments of the plant assemblage at the site and are clearly of different status. Little is known of the use of perishables in the Acheulian material culture, since depositional conditions rarely enable their preservation. The few examples discussed above are the only data available on the perishables and contribute a glimpse of rare items whose existence, even if not understood, should not be neglected.

The number of burned specimens found is very small and no hearths were observed at the site. Consequently, without additional excavations in the area no conclusions regarding the gathering of wood for fire by hominins can be drawn.

Conclusions

The wood assemblage recovered at GBY presents a unique opportunity to investigate the Early/Middle Pleistocene vegetation of the Levant Rift and to reconstruct both the history of the wood accumulation itself and its implications for the ancient geography, environment and ecology of the region. It has direct implications for the habitats in which early hominins were active along the shores of the palaeo-Lake Hula and for the biogeographical corridor which allowed them access to Eurasia from their African homeland.

The present-day vegetation of the Hula Valley has undergone drastic changes through the intervention of man and does not represent the primary vegetation that prevailed during the Pleistocene. Today the area largely comprises cultivated and waste places and the vegetation accordingly consists mainly of segetal and ruderal plants with remnants of the primary vegetation and of *Prosopis farcta* shrubs dispersed among them.

Almost all the species identified in the GBY assemblage are still found in the region today, though in different proportions. Among the wetland vegetation only scattered trees of *Fraxinus syriaca* and *Ulmus canescens* are found today, *Fraxinus syriaca* in Upper Galilee, the Hula Plain, the

Beit Shean Valley and the Golan, and *Ulmus canescens* in Lower Galilee and other more remote locations. Their relatively high percentage in the excavations, especially that of *Fraxinus syriaca*, suggests that these two species constituted in the past the primary forest in the Hula Valley on wetlands or, according to Zohary, primary park forest (Zohary, 1959). Zohary suggested that these species penetrated from the north in one of the more humid intervals of the Quaternary.

Among the dryland vegetation of the Hula Valley, on the flanks of the Golan and Gilead, on the basalt of Korazim and reaching up to the Dan Valley, there are variously dispersed remnants of *Quercus ithaburensis* and *Pistacia atlantica* (Weisel, 1984). Zohary (1959; Zohary and Orshansky, 1947) suggested that these two species constituted a park forest as the primary climax vegetation in these regions. The results of the GBY excavations support the existence of such a forest, open or closed, during the Pleistocene.

Among the excavated wood specimens, *Pistacia atlantica* and *Quercus calliprinos* were found in the oldest layers present at the site. On the other hand, *Ziziphus* was apparently rare in comparison to its abundance today. Its dominance in the valley and on the Korazim basalt is presumably a more recent event following human activity (Weisel, 1984; Zohary, 1959). One genus is extinct in the region today and two species, *Lonicera* and *Rhus*, may perhaps have been replaced by other species of the same genus. On the other hand, there may be higher intraspecific variability than observed up to now.

The identification of *Pistacia vera* is based on its distinction from *P. atlantica* by wood anatomy. The implication that it grew at the time in the region and later became extinct may be rather far-fetched.

A taxon of which many fruits were found in the excavation is *Styrax* (Melamed, 1997), but the fact that no wood of this genus could be identified cannot be explained at this stage of the research.

If driftwood could not have arrived from the north (see Chapter 5), then a few species which grow today only in northern regions (*Cedrus* and *Cerasus*) or are very rare

(*Juniperus oxycedrus* in Upper Galilee) must have grown at the time in the area. Only three specimens of *Juniperus* and two of *Cedrus,* and perhaps two of *Cerasus,* were found. The two segments of *Cedrus* were found in Trench V in Layers V-5 and V-5/6, and the three segments of *Juniperus* in Layers V-6, I-4 and Trench I; all are relatively high layers in the stratigraphic sequence (Table 14).

In addition, the species of *Lonicera* identified here is more similar anatomically to species growing in Europe (Schweingruber, 1990) than to that growing in Israel today. However, the number of specimens found in the excavations is too small to allow any definite conclusions.

The species composition as revealed by the wood assemblage of GBY is not representative of the African floral kingdom but is clearly a Mediterranean one. Therefore, the Acheulian population, which originated in Africa, had at some point during their cultural evolution to adapt to a different environment and ecology, the typically Mediterranean ones portrayed by the analysis of the GBY wood assemblage. It was recently demonstrated that seven fruit-bearing species with hard shells were found in the archaeological horizons of GBY associated with stone assemblages of pitted hammers/anvils. This association, interpreted as evidence for nut consumption by hominins at GBY (Goren-Inbar et al., 2002), is only one aspect within the much wider subject of Mediterranean ecological exploitation. The process of adaptation is beyond the scope of this study and will be dealt with at a later stage of the GBY research. However, as there is little in common between African palaeoecology and that observed at GBY from the botanical perspective, we may conclude that the hominins' habitat was extremely diverse (Goren-Inbar et al., 2000) and represents a rich ecological niche, forming an ideal background for subsistence and exploitation.

Despite the changes in the plant cover and composition in the Hula Valley induced by human activities in the Holocene, and despite the palaeoclimatic oscillations encountered at GBY (Chapter 3; Feibel et al., 1998; Goren-Inbar, in press; Rosenfeld et al., n.d.), it is clear that a great similarity in the composition of arboreal species has existed through the last 780,000 years. This is supported by the recurrence of almost the same taxa throughout the composite profile of the site.

Considering the 34 m thick depositional sequence of the study area as representing an accumulation process of ca. 100 Ka duration (Goren-Inbar et al., 2000), the taxonomic changes of woods, shrubs and climbers from the Early/Middle Pleistocene to the present are minor ones. Worth noting are the observations of Zohary and Orshansky (1947), who reported the abundance of many of the currently rare taxa in the Hula Valley and vicinity some 50 years ago. This may indicate a high degree of resistance and endurance of these species despite the climatic oscillations of the Pleistocene and Holocene. The cyclic nature of the depositional record at the site and the homogeneity of wood taxa as represented in the different strata are indications of a prolonged and continuous stability of an estimated duration of some 100 Ka. This indicates that the drainage system was somewhat similar to the present one, which is characterized by rare events of flash floods (Inbar, 1987; 2000; Inbar et al., 1989; Inbar and Schick, 1979). The amplitude of the climatic oscillations was not pronounced or drastic enough to cause a change in the vegetation of the valley. The wood reflects a continuous and mostly similar drainage configuration that contributed a similar assemblage of driftwood by means of water transport into the shores of the palaeo-Lake Hula. The disappearance of one species that was quite abundant in the excavations should, however, be borne in mind. Its identification, origin and extinction are still enigmatic.

Edible material comprises 37% of the arboreal taxa identified at GBY. Table 21 presents the edible arboreal taxa, listed according to seasonal availability. This material constituted a fraction of the local edible vegetation that could have supported the diet of hominin groups during different seasons. When these data are combined with those derived from the analysis of fruits and seeds, the component of edible material will increase significantly (Melamed, 1997, Goren-Inbar, n.d.). It will further contribute to the attempt to reconstruct the palaeoecology and to understand the attractiveness of the region for the hominins.

110

Table 21: Arboreal plants with edible fruits and seeds and their current manner of usage[*].

Wood Taxon	Fruit Rripening Season	Usage
Amygdalus korschinski	summer	fresh & dry
Cerasus sp.	summer	fresh
Crataegus sp.	end of summer	fresh
Ficus carica	autumn	fresh
Olea europaea	end of summer/autumn	fresh
Pistacia atlantica	autumn	roasted
Pyrus sp.	summer	fresh
Quercus sp.	Winter/autumn	roasted after peeling
Vitis sp.	end of summer/autumn	fresh & dry
Ziziphus sp.	end of summer/autumn	fresh & dry

[*] After Melamed 1997.

The palaeoenvironment of GBY, as it emerges from the analyses of the different disciplines, was an optimal one. Plant diversity was high due to the mosaic of topography and bedrock type. It was associated with a substantial diversity of faunal taxa available to hominin communities that inhabited the valley and its margins. This region also provided diverse raw materials (flint, limestone and basalt) within a minimal distance from the shores of the lake (Delage, n.d.; Goren-Inbar, n.d.; Goren-Inbar et al., 1992; Goren-Inbar and Saragusti, 1996). Moreover, the fauna, flora, raw material availability, climatic conditions and derived seasonality were associated and interrelated with the prolonged presence of a freshwater lake in the Hula Basin (Feibel, 2001; Rosenfeld et al., in press).

The water level of this lake fluctuated during the Pleistocene (and Holocene) between high and low stands. The low stands are represented by coquina layers and the high ones by a variety of mud deposits. The wood assemblages originating in the different layers represent a fairly homogeneous spectrum of taxa throughout the stratigraphic sequence. The high degree of similarity between the Early/Middle Pleistocene taxa and the present-day ones indicates that the fundamental climatic conditions have remained similar since antiquity and that catastrophic events have not distorted the arboreal floral composition in the Hula region. Furthermore, the present-day species grow in a regime of typical long, hot summers and short, wet and cool winters. This regime seems to have

prevailed in antiquity as well, demonstrating an overall and prolonged stability. The unique mosaic phytogeographical configuration of the Hula Valley and its environs has deep roots. This seasonal stability, the chronological continuity of arboreal species (as well as many non-arboreal taxa; Melamed, 1997) and the permanent freshwater body in the valley may all lead to understanding of the mechanism of hominin occupation of the Hula sector of the rift. The stability and permanence of some of the ecological features may explain the repetitive mode of hominin presence along the shores of the palaeo-Lake Hula. Similar patterns are known from the Plio-Pleistocene of the African continent (i.e., Olduvai Gorge, Olorgesailie, East and West Turkana, Middle Awash). The palaeo-Hula record perhaps represents a shorter episode, but nevertheless demonstrates the same pattern: repeated hominin visits to the same geographical locality. This behavioural mode is known from earlier sites in the Dead Sea Rift, such as 'Ubeidiya, where over 70 archaeological occurrences embedded in the 'Ubeidiya Formation of Early Pleistocene age were exposed.

The results obtained from the analysis of wood segments support the view of this assemblage as a driftwood phenomenon, the consequence of a taphonomic process. Clearly, the presence of only a minimal number of shaped or manipulated wood items is not sufficient to indicate patterns of exploitation of this resource by hominins. However, considering the Acheulian material culture and the variety of observed behavioural patterns of these communities, manipulating and using the wood resource was clearly within their abilities. The lack of substantial evidence for hominin involvement may be a result of the particular location of the excavations within the study area. Additional excavations at the site or the application of new methods and techniques of analysis may perhaps yield new data and shed new light on the present interpretation of the taphonomic nature of the wood assemblage.

Great similarity is observed between the African Late Acheulian sites and GBY (Goren-Inbar et al., 2000). The material culture of the latter, currently under investigation, does not indicate substantial differences from that encountered in the African sites. The lithic assemblages, both in Africa and in Southwestern Asia, are characterized by the same techno-typological traits (Clark, 1975) and reflect similar strategies and even tactical patterning. Thus, hominin behaviour with regard to the use of stone

artefacts is independent of any particular environmental setting. The Acheulian techno-complex, culture, tradition or tool-kit prevailed for over 1.5 Ma. The prehistoric communities whose material culture is being studied at GBY did not undergo any visible adaptation to the Early/Middle Pleistocene Mediterranean environment. However, the African plant kingdom is strikingly different from the Mediterranean one. The palaeoclimate, the particularities of the Hula ecosystem and the palaeogeography of that sector of the Dead Sea Rift necessitated some kind of adaptation. It appears that the process of learning was the primary tool by which these hominin populations became familiar with their particular surroundings throughout generations of occupation along the shores of the palaeo-Lake Hula. The study of the wood segments discussed here is only one facet of the great potential for understanding hominin evolution preserved in the waterlogged sediments of the Acheulian site of Gesher Benot Ya'aqov.

References

Adam, K. D. 1951. Der Waldelefant von Lehringen, eine Jagdbeute des diluvial Menschen. *Quartär*, 5:79–92.

Albert, R. M., O. Lavi, L. Estroff, S. Weiner, A. Tsatskin, A. Ronen and S. Lev-Yadun. 1999. Mode of occupation of Tabun Cave, Mt Carmel, Israel during the Mousterian period: a study of the sediments and phytoliths. *Journal of Archaeological Science*, 26:1249–1260.

Albert, R. M., S. Weiner, O. Bar-Yosef and L. Meignen. 2000. Phytoliths in the Middle Palaeolithic deposits of Kebara Cave, Mt Carmel, Israel: study of the plant materials used for fuel and other purposes. *Journal of Archaeological Science*, 27:931–947.

Bamford, M. 1999. Pliocene fossil woods from an early hominid cave deposit, Sterkfontein, South Africa. *South African Journal of Science*, 95:231–238.

Bar-Yosef, O. 1975. Archaeological occurrences in the Middle Pleistocene of Israel. In K. W. Butzer and G. L. Isaac (eds.), *After the Australopithecines: Stratigraphy, Ecology and Culture Change in the Middle Pleistocene*, pp. 571–604. Aldine, Chicago.

Bar-Yosef, O. 1997. Symbolic expressions in later prehistory of the Levant: why are they so few? In M. W. Conkey, O. Soffer, D. Stratmann and N. Jablonski (eds.), *Beyond the Art: Pleistocene Image and Symbol*, Vol. 23, pp. 161–187. California Academy of Sciences, San Francisco.

Bar-Yosef, O., and D. Alon. 1988. *Nahal Hemar Cave*. The Department of Antiquities and Museums, Ministry of Education and Culture, Jerusalem.

Bar-Yosef, O., and N. Goren-Inbar. 1993. *The Lithic Assemblages of 'Ubeidiya*. Qedem 34, Institute of Archaeology, Hebrew University, Jerusalem.

Barbour, R. J., and L. Leney. 1981. ICOM Committee for Conservation, *Waterlogged Wood Working Group*, pp. 209–225. Proceedings of the ICOM Waterlogged Wood Working Group Conference. Ottawa.

Baruch, U., and S. Bottema. 1991. The palynological evidence for climatic changes in the Levant ca. 17,000–9,000 B.P. In O. Bar-Yosef and F. Valla (eds.), *The Natufian Culture in the Levant*, pp. 11–20. International Monographs in Prehistory, Ann Arbor.

—. 1999. A new pollen diagram from Lake Hula: vegetation, climatic, and anthropogenic implications. In H. Kawanabe, G. W. Coulter and A. C. Roosevelt (eds.), *Ancient Lakes: Their Cultural and Biological Diversity*, pp. 75–86. Kenobi Productions, Belgium.

Baruch, U., and N. Goring-Morris. 1997. The arboreal vegetation of the Central Negev Highlands, Israel, at the end of the Pleistocene: evidence from archaeological charred wood remains. *Vegetation History and Archaeobotany*, 6:249–259.

Baruch, U., E. Werker and O. Bar-Yosef. 1992. Charred wood remains from Kebara Cave, Israel: preliminary results. *Bulletin de la Société Botanique de France*, 139:531–538.

Bassinot, F. C., L. D. Labeyrie, E. Vincent, X. Quidelleur, N. J. Shackleton and Y. Lancelot. 1994. The astronomical theory of climate and the age of the Brunhes-Matuyama magnetic reversal. *Earth and Planetary Science Letters*, 126:91–108.

Beaumont, P. 1999. INQUA Excursion B7, Northern Cape. *INQUA, XV International Conference Field Guide*, pp. 1–41.

Department of Archaeology, McGregor Museum, Kimberley.

Belfer-Cohen, A., and N. Goren-Inbar. 1994. Cognition and communication in the Levantine Lower Palaeolithic. *World Archaeology*, 26:144–157.

Belitzky, S. 1987. Tectonics of the Korazim Saddle. M. Sc. thesis, Hebrew University, Jerusalem (in Hebrew).

–. in press Structure and morphotectonics of the Gesher Benot Ya'aqov area, Northern Dead Sea Rift, Israel. *Quaternary Research*.

–. n.d. Paleodrainage and morphotectonic evolution at the Gesher Benot Ya'aqov Bridge area, Northern Dead Sea Rift, Israel.

Belitzky, S., N. Goren-Inbar and E. Werker. 1991. A Middle Pleistocene wooden plank with man-made polish. *Journal of Human Evolution*, 20:349–53.

Biberson, P. 1968. Les gisements acheuléens de Torralba et Ambrona (Espagne): nouvelles précisions. *L'Anthropologie*, 72:241–278.

Birks, H. H. 1980. Plant macrofossils in Quaternary lake sediments. *Archiv Hydrobiologie Beiheft*, 15:1–60.

Boule, M. 1900. Étude paléontologique et archéologique sur la station paléolithique du Lac Karâr (Algérie). *L'Anthropologie*, 11:1–21.

Boyd, W. E. 1988. Methodological problems in the analysis of fossil non-artifactual wood assemblages from archaeological sites. *Journal of Archaeological Science*, 15:603–619.

Braun, D. 1992. The Geology of the Afiquim Area. M. Sc. thesis, Hebrew University, Jerusalem (in Hebrew).

Bridgland, D. R., M. H. Field, J. A. Holmes, J. McNabb, R. C. Preece, I. Selby, J. J. Wymer, S. Boreham, B. G. Irving, S. A. Parfitt and A. J. Stuart. 1999. Middle Pleistocene interglacial Thames-Medway deposits at Clacton-on-Sea, England: reconsideration of the biostratigraphical and environmental context of the type Clactonian Palaeolithic industry. *Quaternary Science Review*, 18:109–146.

Chalk, L., A. C. Hoyle, J. F. Hughes, J. D. Brazier and E. W. J. Phillips. 1969. Provisional identifications of charcoals and wood samples from the Kalambo Falls prehistoric site. In J. D. Clark (ed.), *Kalambo Falls Prehistoric Site*, Vol. I, pp.

218–220. Cambridge University Press, Cambridge.

Clark, J. D. 1969. *Kalambo Falls Prehistoric Site I: The Geography, Paleoecology and Detailed Stratigraphy of the Excavation*. Cambridge University Press, Cambridge.

–. 1970. *The Prehistory of Africa*. Thames & Hudson, London.

–. 1975. A comparison of the Late Acheulian industries of Africa and the Middle East. In K. W. Butzer and G. L. Isaac (eds.), *After the Australopithecines: Stratigraphy, Ecology, and Culture Change in the Middle Pleistocene*, pp. 605–659. Mouton Publishers, The Hague.

–. 2001. Modified, used and other wood and plant specimens from Bwalya Industry Acheulean horizons. In J. D. Clark (ed.), *Kalambo Falls Prehistoric Site*, Vol. III, pp. 481–491. Cambridge University Press, Cambridge.

Cohen, O. 1999. The Kinneret boat: conservation and exhibition. In P. Hoffmann (ed.), *Proceedings of the 7th ICOM-Group on Wet Organic Archaeological Materials*, pp. 182–187. ICOM, Grenoble.

Abacus Concepts. 1992. *StatView*. Abacus Concepts Inc., Berkeley.

Dawson, J. 1981. Some consideration in choosing a biocide. *Proceedings ICOM Waterlogged Wood Working Group Conference*, pp. 269–276. ICOM, Ottawa.

Deacon, H. J. 1970. The Acheulian occupation at Amanzi Springs, Uienhage District, Cape Province. *Annals of the Cape Provincial Museums (Natural History)*, 8:89–189.

Dimentman, C., H. J. Bromley and F. D. Por. 1992. *Lake Hula, Reconstruction of the Fauna and Hydrobiology of a Lost Lake*. Israel Academy of Sciences and Humanities, Jerusalem.

Echegaray, J. G., and L. G. Freeman. 1998. *La Paléolithique inférieur et moyen en Espagne*. Jérôme Millon, Grenoble.

Fahn, A., E. Werker and P. Bass. 1986. *Wood Anatomy and Identification of Trees and Shrubs from Israel and Adjacent Regions*. Israel Academy of Sciences and Humanities, Jerusalem.

Feibel, C. S. 2001. Archaeological sediments in lake margin environments. In J. K. Stein and W. R. Farrand (eds.), *Sediments in Archaeological Context*, pp. 103–118. University of Utah Press, Salt Lake City.

Feibel, C. S., N. Goren-Inbar, K. L. Verosub and I. Saragusti.

1998. Gesher Benot Ya'aqov, Israel: new evidence for its stratigraphic and sedimentologic context. *Journal of Human Evolution*, 34:A7.

Feinbrun-Dothan, N. 1978. *Flora Palaestina*. Israel Academy of Sciences and Humanities, Jerusalem.

Florian, M.-L. E. 1990. Scope and history of archaeological wood. In M. Rowell and R. B. Barbour (eds.), *Archaeological Wood Properties, Chemistry, and Preservation*, pp. 3–23. American Chemical Society, Washington DC.

Forest, H. H. D. 1894. Notes of a tour in Mount Lebanon, and to the eastern side of Lake Hûleh. *Journal of the American Oriental Society*, 2:235–247.

Freeman, L. G. 1975. Acheulian sites and stratigraphy in Iberia and the Maghreb. In K. W. Butzer and G. L. Isaac (eds.), *After the Australopithecines: Stratigraphy, Ecology and Culture Change in the Middle Pleistocene*, pp. 661–744. Aldine, Chicago.

Gafny, S. 1992. The Effect of Substrate Type on the Structure and Function of the Littoral Zone of Lake Kinneret. Ph. D. thesis, Tel Aviv University, Tel Aviv (in Hebrew).

Gale, R., and D. Cutler. 2000. *Plants in Archaeology – Identification, Manual of Artefacts of Plant Origin from Europe and the Mediterranean*. Westbury & Royal Botanic Gardens, Kew.

Gat, Z., and Z. Paster. 1974. *Agroclimate of the Golan Heights: The Rain*. Israel Meteorological Service, Bet Dagan.

—. 1975. *Agroclimate of the Golan Heights: Temperatures and Relative Humidity*. Israel Meteorological Service, Bet Dagan.

Gaudzinski, S. 1996. *Kärlich-Seeufer. Untersuchungen zu einer altpaläolithischen Fundstelle im Neuwieder Becken (Rheinland-Pfalz)*. Römisch-Germanischen Zentralmuseums Mainz, Mainz.

—. 1999. Considerations on the taphonomy of the faunal assemblage from the Middle Pleistocene Kärlich-Seeufer site (Central Rhineland, Germany). In *The Role of Early Humans in the Accumulation of European Lower and Middle Palaeolithic Bone Assemblages*, Vol. 42, pp. 139–152. Römisch-Germanisches Zentralmuseum Forschungsinstitut für Vor- und Frühgeschichte, Mainz.

Gaudzinski, S., F. Bittmann, W. Boenigk, M. Frechen and T. V.

Kolfschoten. 1996. Palaeoecology and archaeology of the Kärlich-Seeufer open-air site (Middle Pleistocene) in the central Rhineland, Germany. *Quaternary Research*, 46:319–334.

Geraads, D., and E. Tchernov. 1983. Fémurs humains du Pléistocène moyen de Gesher Benot Ya'aqov (Israël). *L'Anthropologie*, 87:138–141.

Gilead, D. 1968. Gesher Benot Ya'aqov. *Hadashot Archeologiot*, 27:34–35 (in Hebrew).

—. 1970. Handaxe industries in Israel and the Near East. *World Archaeology*, 2:1–11.

Goren-Inbar, N. 1992. The Acheulian site of Gesher Benot Ya'aqov – an Asian or an African entity? In T. Akazawa, K. Aoki and T. Kimura (eds.), *The Evolution and Dispersal of Modern Humans in Asia*, pp. 67–82. Hokusen-sha, Tokyo.

—. 1998. Gesher Benot Ya'aqov: the Acheulian cultural sequence. *Journal of Human Evolution*, 34:A8.

—. n.d. The Gesher Benot Ya'aqov Acheulian site – environment and behaviour of the Early/Middle Pleistocene settlers in the Hula Valley.

Goren-Inbar, N., and S. Belitzky. 1989. Structural position of the Pleistocene Gesher Benot Ya'aqov site in the Dead Sea Rift zone. *Quaternary Research*, 31:371–376.

Goren-Inbar, N., S. Belitzky, K. Verosub, E. Werker, M. Kislev, A. Heimann, I. Carmi and A. Rosenfeld. 1992a. New discoveries at the Middle Pleistocene Gesher Benot Ya'aqov Acheulian site. *Quaternary Research*, 38:117–128.

Goren-Inbar, N., S. Belitzky, Y. Goren, R. Rabinovitch and I. Saragusti. 1992b. Gesher Benot Ya'aqov – the 'bar': an Acheulian assemblage. *Geoarchaeology*, 7:27–40.

Goren-Inbar, N., C. S. Feibel, K. L. Verosub, Y. Melamed, M. E. Kislev, E. Tchernov and I. Saragusti. 2000. Pleistocene milestones on the Out-of-Africa Corridor at Gesher Benot Ya'aqov, Israel. *Science*, 289:944–974.

Goren-Inbar, N., A. Lister, E. Werker and M. Chech. 1994. A butchered elephant skull and associated artifacts from the Acheulian site of Gesher Benot Ya'aqov, Israel. *Paléorient*, 20:99–112.

Goren-Inbar, N., and I. Saragusti. 1996. An Acheulian biface assemblage from the site of Gesher Benot Ya'aqov, Israel: indications of African affinities. *Journal of Field*

Archaeology, 23:15–30.

Goren-Inbar, N., G. Sharon, Y. Melamed and M. Kislev. 2002. Nuts, nut cracking, and pitted stones at Gesher Benot Ya'aqov, Israel. *Proceedings National Academy of Science, USA.*

Greguss, P. 1955. *Xylotomische Bestimmung der heute lebenden Gymnospermen.* Akadémiai Kiadó, Budapest.

—. 1959. *Holzanatomie der europäischen Laubhölzer und Sträucher.* Akadémiai Kidaó, Budapest.

Grundwag, M., and E. Werker. 1976. Comparative wood anatomy as an aid to identification of *Pistacia* L. species. *Israel Journal of Botany*, 25:152–167.

Hartman, A. 1997. Landscape and Agriculture of the Carmel Coastal Plain in the PPNC Period. M. A. thesis, Bar-Ilan University, Ramat-Gan (in Hebrew).

Hodges, L. E., and J. D. Clark. 1969. List of useful plants, trees and shrubs collected in the immediate vicinity of the Kalambo Falls local basin in 1956. In J. D. Clark (ed.), *Kalambo Falls Prehistoric Site*, Vol. I, pp. 228–229. Cambridge University Press, Cambridge.

Hoffman, P. 1986. On the stabilization of waterlogged oakwood with PEG, II: designing a two-step treatment for multi-quality timber. *Studies in Conservation*, 31:103–113.

Hoffman, P., and M. A. Jones. 1990. Structure and degradation process for waterlogged archaeological wood. In M. Rowell and R. B. Barbour (eds.), *Archaeological Wood Properties, Chemistry, and Preservation*, pp. 35–65. American Chemical Society, Washington DC.

Horowitz, A. 1973. Development of the Hula Basin, Israel. *Israel Journal of Earth Sciences*, 22:107–139.

—. 1979. *The Quarternary of Israel.* Academic Press, New York.

—. 1989. Continuous pollen diagrams for the last 3.5 M.Y. from Israel: vegetation, climate and correlation with the oxygen isotope record. *Palaeogeography, Palaeoclimatology, Palaeoecology*, 72:63–78.

—. 2001. *The Jordan Rift Valley.* A. A. Balkema Publishers, Lisse.

Howell, F. C. 1966. Observations on the earlier phases of the European Lower Paleolithic. *American Anthropologist*, 68:88–201.

Inbar, M. 1987. Effects of high magnitude flood in a Mediterranean climate: a case study in the Jordan River basin. In L. Mayer and D. Nash (eds.), *Catastrophic Flooding*, pp. 333–353. Allen & Unwin, Boston.

—. 2000. Episodes of flash-floods and boulder transport in the Upper Jordan River. In M. Hassan, O. Slaymaker and S. Berkowicz (eds.), *The Hydrology-Geomorphology Interface: Rainfall, Floods, Sedimentation, Land Use. International Assocociation of Hydrological Sciences*, No. 261, pp. 185-200. Oxfordshire UK Publications, Wallingford.

Inbar, M., Y. Bartov and V. Arad. 1989. *Hula Valley and Korazim Region, Bibliography of Geological Research.* Ministry of Energy and Infrastructure, Geological Survey of Israel, Jerusalem.

Inbar, M., and A. P. Schick. 1979. Bedload transport associated with high stream power, Jordan River, Israel. *Proceedings National Academy of Science, USA, Geology*, 76:2525–2517.

Irby, C. L., and J. Mangles. 1844. *Travels in Egypt and Nubia, Syria and the Holy Land; Including a Journey Round the Dead Sea, and through the Country East of the Jordan.* John Murray, London.

Jacob-Friesen, K. H. 1956. Eiszeitliche elefantenjäger in der Lüneburger Heide. *Jahrbuch des Römische-Germanischen Zentralmuseums*, 3:1–22.

Karmon, Y. 1953. The settlement of the Northern Huleh Valley since 1838. *Israel Exploration Journal*, 3:4–25.

—. 1956. *The Northern Huleh Valley: Its Natural and Cultural Landscape.* Magness Press, Hebrew University, Jerusalem.

—. 1960. The drainage of the Huleh swamps. *Geographical Review*, 50:169–193.

Kim, Y. S., and A. P. Singh. 2000. Micromorphological characteristics of wood biodegradation in wet environments: a review. *International Association of Wood Anatomists*, 21:135–155.

Kislev, M., and Y. Melamed. in press. Botanical and archaeobotanical evidence from Israel for grape domestication, *Xth Symposium of the International Workgroup for Botany*, Innsbruck.

Klein, C. 1961. *On the Fluctuations of the Level of the Dead Sea since the Beginning of the 19th Century.* Hydrological Service, Ministry of Agriculture, Jerusalem.

—. 1982. Morphological evidence of lake level changes, western shore of the Dead Sea. *Israel Journal of Earth*

Sciences, 31:67–94.

Lev, E. 1992. The Vegetal Food of the "Neanderthal" Man in Kebara Cave, Mt. Carmel in the Middle Palaeolithic Period. M. Sc. thesis, Bar-Ilan University, Ramat-Gan (in Hebrew).

Lev-Yadun, S. and R. Aloni. 1990. Vascular differentiation in branch junctions of trees: circular patterns and functional significance. *Trees*, 4:49-54.

Lev-Yadun, S., M. Artzy, E. Marcus and R. Stidsing. 1996. Wood remains from Tel Nami, a Middle Bronze IIa and Late Bronze IIb port: exploitation of trees and Levantine cedar trade. *Economic Botany*, 50:310–317.

Light, J. P. 2001. Non-Destructive XRF Sourcing of Basaltic Artifacts from Gesher Benot Ya'aqov, Israel: Implications for Hominid Behavior. M. Sc. thesis, University of California, Davis.

Light, J. P., K. L. Verosub and N. Goren-Inbar. 1999. Sourcing of Basaltic Artifacts from the Gesher Benot Ya'aqov Archaeological Site, Israel: Raw Material Selection and Hominid Behavior, *INQUA XV*, Durban, South Africa.

Liphschitz, N. 1986. The vegetational landscape and macroclimate of Israel during prehistoric and protohistoric periods. *Mitekufat Haeven*, 19:80*–89*.

—. 1990. Nophei hazomeach hativi shel emeq hahula beavar. In G. Bigger and E. Schiler (eds.), *Emeq Hahula Usvivato*, pp. 75–76. Ariel, Jerusalem (in Hebrew).

Liphschitz, N., and D. Nadel. 1997. Charred wood remains from Ohalo II (19,000 B.P.), Sea of Galilee, Israel. *Mitekufat Haeven*, 27:5–18.

Lorch, J. 1966. A Pleistocene florule from the Central Jordan Valley. *Israel Journal of Botany*, 15:31–34.

Mania, D. 1988. Le Paléolithique ancien et moyen de la région de la Saale et de l'Elbe, Allemagne de l'Est. *L'Anthropologie*, 92:1051–1091.

Matsutani, A. 1987. Plant remains from the 1984 excavations at Douara Cave. In T. Akazawa and Y. Sakaguchi (eds.), *Paleolithic site of Douara Cave*, Bulletin no. 21, pp. 117–122. Tokyo University, Tokyo.

McGregor, J. 1870. *The Rob Roy on the Jordan, Nile, Redsea, & Gennesareth, &c. A Canoe Cruise in Palestine and Egypt, and the Waters of Damascus*. 2nd edition. John Murray, London.

McNabb, J. 1989. Sticks and stones: a possible experimental solution to the question of how the Clacton spear point was made. *Proceedings of the Prehistoric Society*, 55:251–257.

Melamed, Y. 1997. Reconstruction of the Landscape and the Vegetarian Diet at Gesher Benot Ya'aqov Archaeological Site in the Lower Paleolithic Period. M. Sc. thesis, Bar-Ilan University (in Hebrew).

Mikesell, M. W. 1969. The deforestation of Mount Lebanon. *The Geographical Review*, 59:1–28.

Movius, H. L. 1950. A wooden spear of third interglacial age from Lower Saxony. *Southwestern Journal of Anthropology*, 6:139–142.

Nadel, D., and E. Werker. 1999. The oldest ever brush hut plant remains from Ohalo II, Jordan Valley, Israel (19,000 BP). *Antiquity*, 73:755–764.

Neuville, R. 1951. *Le Paléolithique et le Mésolithique du désert du Judée*. Massons et CIE, éditeurs, Paris.

Oakley, K. P., P. Andrews, L. H. Keeley and J. D. Clark. 1977. A reappraisal of the Clacton spearpoint. *Proceedings of the Prehistoric Society*, 43:13–30.

Pétrequin, P., and A.-M. Pétrequin. 1993. *Écologie d'un outil: la hache de pierre en Irian Jaya (Indonésie)*. Éditions CNRS, Paris.

Picard, L. 1952. The Pleistocene peat of Lake Hula. *Bulletin of the Research Council of Israel*, G2:147–156.

Rabinovitch-Vin, A. 1977. The vegetation of the Lower Galilee. In U. Paz (ed.), *Studies and Surveys in Nature Preservation in Israel*, Vol. 2. Nature Reserves Authority, Jerusalem.

—. 1986. *Parent Rock, Soil and Vegetation in Galilee*. Nature Reserves Authority and Kibbutz Hameuchad Publishing House Ltd., Tel-Aviv.

Robinson, E. 1865. *Physical Geography of the Holy Land*. John Murray, London.

Rosenfeld, A., Y. Nathan, C. S. Feibel, B. Shilman, L. Halicz, N. Goren-Inbar and R. Siman-Tov. in press. Paleoenvironment of the Acheulian Gesher Benot Ya'aqov Pleistocene lacustrine strata, Northern Israel – lithology, ostracod assemblages and ostracod shell geochemistry. *Palaeogeography, Palaeclimatology, Palaeoecology*.

Rowell, R. M., and R. J. Barbour. 1990. *Archaeological Wood*

Properties, Chemistry, and Preservation. American Chemical Society, Washington.

Sakai, H. 1991. Process of deterioration of buried wood. *Mokuzai Gakkaishi*, 37:363–369.

Schick, T. 1998. *The Cave of the Warrior, a Fourth Millennium Burial in the Judean Desert.* Israel Antiquities Authority Report, No. 5, Jerusalem.

Schweingruber, H. F. 1990. *Anatomy of European Woods.* Haupt, Stuttgart.

Sharon, G., C. S. Feibel, S. Belitzky, O. Marder, H. Khalaily and R. Rabinovich. in press. The drainage destruction at Gesher Benot Ya'aqov 1999: archaeological, geological and ecological implications. *'Atiqot.*

Simchoni, O. 1998. Reconstruction of the Landscape and Human Economy 19,000 BP in the Upper Jordan Valley by the Botanical Remains Found at Ohalo II. Ph. D. thesis, Bar Ilan University, Ramat-Gan (in Hebrew).

Spicer, R. A. 1989. The formation and interpretation of plant fossil assemblages. In J. A. Callow (ed.), *Advances in Botanical Research*, pp. 95–191. Academic Press, London.

—. 1991. Plant taphonomic processes. In P. A. Allison and D. E. G. Briggs (eds.), *Taphonomy: Releasing the Data Locked in the Fossil Record*, pp. 71–113. Plenum Press, New York.

Spicer, R. A., and J. A. Wolfe. 1987. Plant taphonomy of late Holocene deposits in Trinity (Clair Engle) Lake, northern California. *Paleobiology*, 13:227–245.

Stekelis, M. 1960. The Paleolithic deposits of Jisr Banat Yaqub. *Bulletin of the Research Council of Israel*, G9:61–87.

Stekelis, M., L. Picard, and D. M. A. Bate. 1937. Jisr Banat Ya'qub. *Quarterly of the Department of Antiquities, Palestine*, 6:214–215.

—. 1938. Jisr Banat Ya'qub. *Quarterly of the Department of Antiquities, Palestine*, 7:45.

Stiner, M. C., S. L. Kuhn, S. Weiner and O. Bar-Yosef. 1995. Differential burning, recrystallization, and fragmentation of archaeological bone. *Journal of Archaeological Science*, 22:223–237.

Tchernov, E. 1973. On the Pleistocene molluscs of the Jordan Valley. *Proceedings of the Israel Academy of Sciences and Humanities*, 11:1–46.

—. 1986. *Les mammifères du Pléistocène inférieur de la Vallée du Jordain à Oubeidiyeh.* Association Paléorient, Paris.

—. 1987. The age of the Ubeidiya Formation, an early Pleistocene hominid site in the Jordan Valley, Israel. *Israel Journal of Earth Sciences*, 36:3–30.

—. 1988. The paleobiogeographical history of the southern Levant. In Y. Yom-Tov and E. Tchernov (eds.), *The Zoogeography of Israel*, pp. 159–250. Dr. W. Junk Publishers, The Hague.

—. 1992. Biochronology, paleoecology, and dispersal events of hominids in the southern Levant. In T. Akazawa, K. Aoki and T. Kimura (eds.), *The Evolution and Dispersal of Modern Humans in Asia*, pp. 149–188. Hokusen-sha, Tokyo.

Thieme, H. 1996. Altpaläolithische Wurfspeere aus Schöningen, Niedersachsen, ein Vorbeicht. *Römische-Germanisches Zentralmuseum*, 26:377–393.

—. 1997. Lower Palaeolithic hunting spears from Germany. *Nature*, 385:807–810.

—. 1999. Altpaläolithische Holzgeräte aus Schöningen, Lkr. Helmstedt. Bedeutsame Funde zur Kulturentwicklung des frühen Menschen. *Germania*, 77:451–487.

Thieme, H., and S. Veil. 1985. Neue Untersuchungen zum eemzeitlichen Elefanten–Jagdplatz Lehringen, Ldkr. Verden. *Die Kunde*, 36 (N. F.):11–58.

Thomas, H. 1985. The early and middle Miocene land connection of the Afro-Arabian plate and Asia: a major event in hominoid dispersal? In E. Delson (ed.), *Ancestors: The Hard Evidence*, pp. 42–50. A.R. Liss, New York.

Tobias, P. 1966. *A Member of the Genus Homo from 'Ubeidiya.* Israel Academy of Sciences and Humanities, Jerusalem.

Tristram, H. B. 1876. *The Land of Israel: A Journal of Travels in Palestine (Undertaken with Special Reference to its Physical Character).* Revised 3rd edition. Society for Promoting Christian Knowledge, London.

—. 1887. *Natural History of the Bible: a Review of the Physical Geography, Geology and Meteorology of the Holy Land.* 5th ed. Scociety for Promoting Christian Knowledge, London.

Tydesley, J. A., and P. G. Bahn. 1983. Use of plants in the European Palaeolithic: a review of the evidence.

Quaternary Science Reviews, 2:53–81.

Verosub, K. L., N. Goren-Inbar, C. S. Feibel and I. Saragusti. 1998. Location of the Matuyama/Brunhes boundary in the Gesher Benot Ya'aqov archaeological site. *Journal of Human Evolution*, 34:A22.

Vin, A. 1977. The vegetation of the Lower Galilee. In U. Paz (ed.), *Studies and Surveys in Nature Preservation in Israel*, Vol. 2. Nature Reserves Authority, Jerusalem.

Warnock, P. 1998. From plant domestication to phytoliths interpretation: the history of paleoethnobotany in the Near East. *Near Eastern Archaeology*, 61:238–252.

Weiner, S., S. Schiegl, P. Goldberg and O. Bar-Yosef. 1995. Mineral assemblages in Kebara and Hayonim Caves, Israel: excavation strategies, bone preservation, and wood ash remnants. *Israel Journal of Chemistry*, 35:143–154.

Weisel, Y. 1984. Vegetation of Israel. In A. Alon (ed.), *Plants and Animals of the Land of Israel: An Illustrated Encyclopedia*, Vol. 8, pp. 172–179. Ministry of Defence/The Publishing House, Society for Protection of Nature, Israel, Tel-Aviv (in Hebrew).

Wells, M. J. 1970. Plant remains from Amanzi Springs. *Annals of the Cape Provincial Museums (Natural History)*, 8:191–194.

Werker, E. 1998. Plant identification of the wooden objects. In T. Schick (ed.), *The Cave of the Warrior, a Fourth Millennium Burial in the Judean Desert*, pp. 92–96. Israel Antiquities Authority Report, No. 5, Jerusalem.

Werker, E., and N. Goren-Inbar. 2001. Reconstruction of the woody vegetation at the Acheulian site of Gesher Benot Ya'aqov, Dead Sea Rift, Israel. In B. A. Purdy (ed.), *Enduring Records: The Environmental and Cultural Heritage of Wetlands*, pp. 206–213. Oxbow Books, Oxford.

Wheeler, E. A., and P. Bass. 1998. Wood identification – a review. *International Association of Wood Anatomy Journal*, 19:241–264.

Wheeler, E. A., R. G. Pearson, C. A. LaPasha, T. Zak, and W. Hatley. 1986. *Computer-Aided Wood Identification*. North Carolina Agricultural Research Service, Bull. 474, North Carolina State University, Raleigh.

White, F. 1969. Identification of fruits and seeds from Site B, Kalambo Falls. In J. D. Clark (ed.), *Kalambo Falls Prehistoric Site*, Vol. I, pp. 216–217. Cambridge University Press, Cambridge.

Whitmore, T. C. 1969. Report on bark and other specimens from site B, Kalambo Falls, depositional phase F2, white sands beds, Mkamba Member (associated with Upper Acheulian artifacts on Occupation Surfaces V and VI, Excavations B1 and B2, 1959. In J. D. Clark (ed.), *Kalambo Falls Prehistoric Site*, Vol. I, pp. 221–224. Cambridge University Press, Cambridge.

Zohary, D., and P. Spiegel-Roy. 1975. Beginnings of fruit growing in the Old World. *Science*, 187:319–327.

Zohary, M. 1959. *Geobotany*. Sifriat Hapoalim, Merhavia (in Hebrew).

—. 1960. The maquis of *Quercus calliprinos* in Israel and Jordan. *Bulletin of the Research Council of Israel*, D9: 51–72.

—. 1962. *Plant Life of Palestine: Israel and Jordan*. Roland Press Company, New York.

—. 1966. *Flora Palaestina*, Vol. 1. Israel Academy of Sciences and Humanities, Jerusalem.

—. 1972. *Flora Palaestina*, Vol. 2. Israel Academy of Sciences and Humanities, Jerusalem.

—. 1980. *Vegetal Landscapes of Israel*. Am Oved, Tel Aviv (in Hebrew).

—. 1982. *Plants of the Bible*. Cambridge University Press, Cambridge.

Zohary, M., and G. Orshansky. 1947. The vegetation of the Huleh Plain. *Palestine Journal of Botany (Jerusalem Series)*, 4:90–104.

Appendix

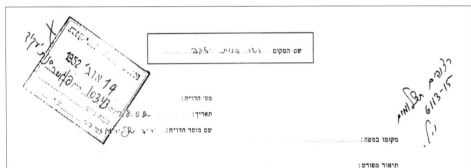

Appendix 1: Mr. Yariv Shapira's report to the Department of Antiquities.